Winning S

A Twelve-Week Plan for Preparing Your NIH Phase II Application

Eva Garland Consulting, LLC

Copyright © 2018 Eva Garland Consulting, LLC
All Rights Reserved

ISBN: 1727735145
ISBN-13: 978-1727735147

CONTENTS

INTRODUCTION i

ACKNOWLEDGEMENTS ix

I. COMMERCIALIZATION PLAN 1
    1. Review the requirements of the Commercialization Plan and initiate tasks with long lead times.
    2. Conduct market research.
    3. Write your Commercialization Plan.
    4. Obtain feedback from experts.
    5. Complete the final draft of your Commercialization Plan.

II. RESEARCH PLAN 30
    1. Define the scope of your Phase II project and initiate long lead-time items.
    2. Perform a current literature search.
    3. Write the Specific Aims page.
    4. Prepare the first draft of your Research Strategy.
    5. Obtain feedback from experts.
    6. Complete the final draft of your Research Plan.

III. OTHER COMPONENTS 46
    1. Check company registrations.
    2. Complete administrative information in the application package.
    3. Prepare other components.
    4. Submit Proposal!

IV. REVIEW AND AWARD PROCESS 79
    1. Navigate the review process.
    2. Prepare a resubmission, if necessary.
    3. Receive your Notice of Award! Understand your company's Phase II responsibilities.
    4. Prepare for "beyond Phase II."

GLOSSARY OF ABBREVIATIONS 99

INDEX 101

INTRODUCTION

If you are reading this book, you are likely within the select group of companies who have been awarded a National Institutes of Health (NIH) Phase I Small Business Innovation Research (SBIR) or Small Business Technology Transfer (STTR) grant. Congratulations on this achievement, and welcome to the "Big Leagues" of preparing a Phase II application!

As an NIH Program Officer (PO) once told us, "The purpose of your Phase I project is to get to Phase II!" There is substantial wisdom in this experienced PO's advice. Your Phase I award likely provided you with just enough funding (generally $150K-$300K) to complete a proof-of-concept study. Phase II awards, which are much larger in total costs (generally $1.5M - $3M), can fund a significant portion of your subsequent development needs. In some cases, Phase II funding will support pre-clinical studies that will enable you to file an Investigational New Drug (IND) or Investigational Device Exemption (IDE) application at the end of the project. In other cases, your Phase II award can fund clinical work, manufacturing scale-up, or advanced software development.

Given the much larger dollar amounts available in Phase II compared to Phase I, it is not surprising that substantially more time will be required to prepare your Phase II application compared to your Phase I application. Whereas preparation of your first Phase I proposal likely required 100 - 150 hours, you will need to set aside approximately 300 hours to prepare your Phase II application. It can take several months to complete the tasks necessary for assembling a competitive Phase II proposal, such as preparing a regulatory plan and developing relationships with investors and partners. It is therefore a good idea to start preparing your Phase II proposal early during your Phase I project period.

In addition to the proposal elements that you are familiar with from your Phase I application (Specific Aims, Research Strategy, Biographical Sketches, Budget, etc.), the Phase II application requires a Progress Report and a Commercialization Plan. The Progress Report is part of the 12-page Research Strategy, and it describes the results of your Phase I project. The Commercialization Plan is a 12-page document that outlines a logical pathway for successfully launching and profiting from your product. In addition, there is increased emphasis on the "optional" Letters of Support in Phase II. Reviewers will expect letters that confirm the commercial potential of your technology from key opinion leaders, customers, and other stakeholders.

The previous book in this series presented a linear timeline for preparing your Phase I application. For Phase II, you will not be able to write your application using a linear approach, as you will need to work on several tasks in parallel. It is therefore important to be highly organized to ensure all tasks are completed in time for the Phase II submission deadline. This is, of course, in addition to running your company, finishing your Phase I research, and ensuring that you comply with the terms of your Phase I award!

Keys to a successful Phase II application

As you embark on your journey to prepare your Phase II application, keep in mind the following key points:

1) **Budget requirements.** For a Phase II SBIR application, 50% of the total budget must be used for internal expenses. This contrasts with Phase I SBIR applications, for which 67% of the

total budget must be used for internal expenses. The more lenient requirement for the Phase II application will enable you to outsource more development work. For STTR applications, the requirements remain the same as for Phase I, with at least 40% of the budget directed to the company, at least 30% directed to the Partnering Research Institution, and the remaining funds allocated to the company, the Partnering Research Institution, third parties, or a combination thereof.

2) **Resubmission guidelines.** You are allowed to submit an initial Phase II application and, if necessary, a single resubmission, called an "A1." If your initial submission and resubmission are not funded, you cannot submit any further Phase II applications for that project. At that point, you may start over with a new Phase I or Fast-Track application. The importance of receiving funding for your Phase II project within the first two submission attempts underscores the need to put in your best effort on each submission.

3) **Timeline for submission.** Phase II applications must be submitted no later than 6 submission cycles after the end of your Phase I project period (approximately 2 years, since there are 3 receipt dates per year). Make sure that you pay attention to the last date on which you are eligible to submit your Phase II proposal so that you don't miss the deadline. Importantly, no-cost extensions (NCEs) do not extend the Phase II submission deadline.

4) **Eligibility.** Many companies receive additional financing during their Phase I project period from outside equity investors. Ensure you are still eligible for SBIR/STTR awards by meeting the company ownership requirements. In some cases, a company that receives equity financing may no longer be eligible for an

STTR, but would be eligible for an SBIR. The NIH allows you to switch between the STTR and SBIR mechanisms between Phase I and Phase II, and this can be a helpful way to meet the eligibility requirements as well as to structure the proposal to meet your product development needs.

5) **Transition between Phase I and Phase II.** To reduce the gap in funding between the Phase I and Phase II programs, you should initiate preparation of your Phase II application while you are carrying out your Phase I research. The process of preparing a Phase II application will require a significant amount of multi-tasking and coordination among both your business and scientific teams. By submitting your Phase II application at the earliest possible due date, you can receive your Phase II funding more quickly, enabling you to keep the momentum going on your product development.

6) **Review process.** The same Special Emphasis Scientific Review Group (SRG) that reviewed your Phase I application will likely review your Phase II proposal. Many SRGs allot more time to the discussion of Phase II and Fast-Track proposals than Phase I applications during the Panel Review, so your proposal will likely be more closely scrutinized in the Phase II review process. In addition, Phase II reviewers will have access to your Phase I Summary Statement, and some reviewers may even remember reviewing your Phase I proposal, so make sure you have addressed all reviewer critiques from your Phase I application!

As with your Phase I application, the SRG assigned to your proposal will evaluate your project based on 5 review criteria: Significance, Innovation, Approach, Investigators, and Environment. For Phase II, reviewers will also evaluate your

Phase I Progress Report and your Commercialization Plan. Competitive proposals will address the following:

Significance: Your technology must address a well-described and supported unmet need. In Phase II, you should have a more specific vision for the sector of the market that your product will address, as well as a clear plan for how it will impact human health.

Innovation: Your technology must be highly differentiated from other approaches. In Phase II, it is important to emphasize not only that your technology is different from other approaches, but that it is better positioned to uniquely solve a well-defined problem.

Approach: Your proposal should present a clear development plan that logically follows from where your Phase I program concluded. Your Phase II plan of work should focus more on the "development" side of "R&D," whereas in Phase I, you may still have been addressing some basic research questions. It is important for your Phase II SBIR/STTR application to advance your technology "vertically" toward commercialization rather than "horizontally" in developing broader scientific knowledge.

Investigators: In Phase II, your team should consist of a mix of scientific, product development, and business experts. Include individuals with experience in commercializing products in your field to demonstrate that you have a team that is capable of effectively developing your product for its intended market.

Environment: As with Phase I, you should clearly describe company facilities and/or access to facilities at partnering institutions or contract research organizations (CROs) that are appropriately equipped to carry out the proposed studies.

Commercial Potential: A critical aspect of your Phase II application will be a well-developed Commercialization Plan that details a realistic path to market. It is also important to include Letters of Support from potential industry partners, investors, and key opinion leaders that validate the information that you include in your Commercialization Plan.

The objective of this book is to assist you with preparing an application that will score highly in each of the above review criteria.

Gearing up for your Phase II application

Before you start working through the tasks in this book, download the latest version of the Application Guide, which is entitled: "SBIR/STTR INSTRUCTIONS FOR NIH AND OTHER PHS AGENCIES." We will refer to these instructions frequently throughout this book.

Our Phase I book was organized such that each chapter corresponded to a different week in the proposal preparation process. Given the additional complexity of the Phase II application, we have segmented this book by major components of the Phase II application to provide you with a useful organizational structure for preparing your proposal. The first three sections of the book are: Commercialization Plan (Section I); Research Plan (Section II); and Other Components (Section III). Each of these sections provides a suggested list of tasks to complete over a 12-week period, offering a logical progression for completing your proposal. In Section IV, we cover the Review and Award Process from the time that you submit your Phase II proposal until you successfully receive funding.

An overview of the suggested timeline for preparing each component of the proposal is provided on page viii. We recommend that you review these suggested timelines, compare them with your company's calendar, and make any modifications necessary to accommodate time needed to complete your Phase I research project and to conduct other company priorities. Be sure to also account for vacations and holidays that may slow down communication with collaborators, contractors, and potential partners.

The guidance in this book is intended to provide you with a smooth and efficient structure for developing your Phase II proposal. By following the suggested timelines, you will be ready to submit your Phase II proposal in approximately 12 weeks!

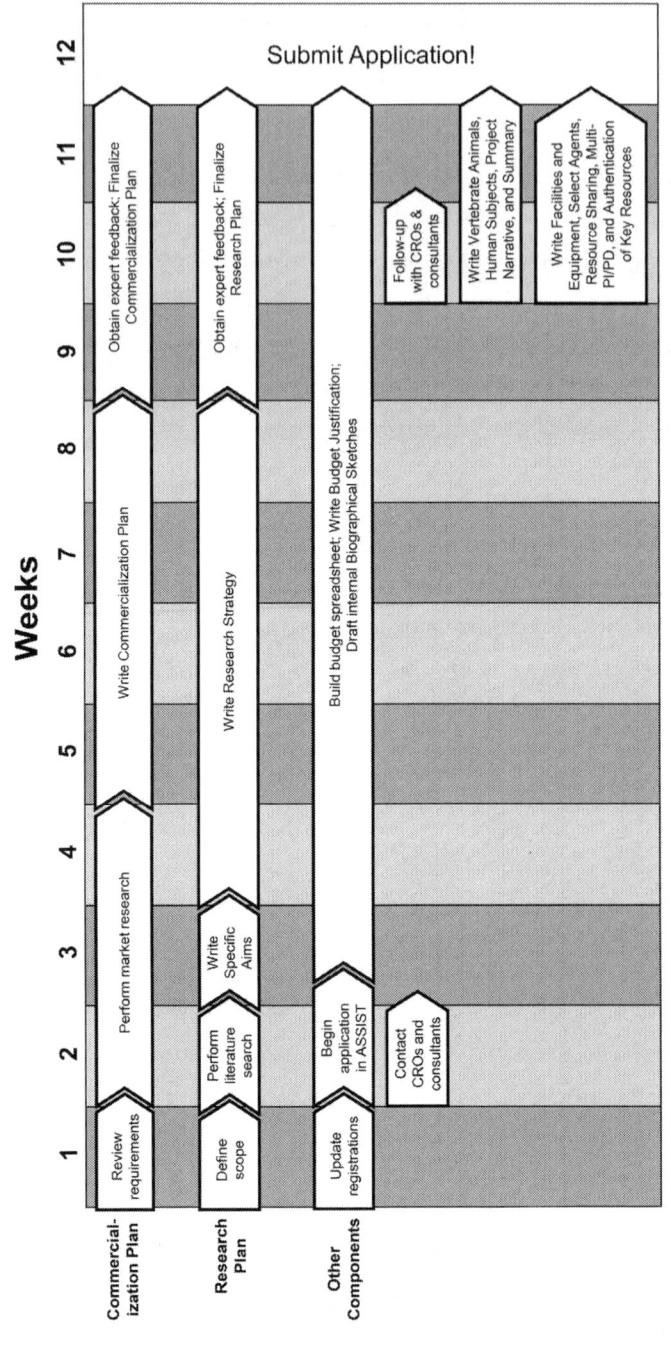

Suggested timeline for preparing a Phase II SBIR/STTR proposal.

ACKNOWLEDGEMENTS

In our decades working with the NIH SBIR/STTR program, we have had the privilege to interact with an extraordinary team of individuals at the NIH. For a program that awards nearly two thousand grants each year with an overall budget of several hundred million dollars to function so smoothly is a testament to the leadership of the NIH SBIR/STTR program, which is currently under the guidance of Program Coordinator Matt Portnoy. Dr. Portnoy is both a highly approachable and effective leader, and we have been grateful for the assistance he has provided to our team and to hundreds of our clients. We are also highly appreciative of the wonderful group of deeply committed Program Officers, Scientific Review Officers, and Grants Management Specialists who have provided guidance and support to thousands of NIH SBIR/STTR applicants and awardees.

We have taken a highly collaborative approach to writing this book, drawing on the expertise of our Scientific Consultants, Grant Writing Specialists, and Compliance Team who have a combined 100+ years of experience writing SBIR/STTR grants. The majority of the text was written by Eva Garland, Ph.D. and Angela Pollard, Ph.D. We thank Rebekah Fleming, Ph.D., Tara Miele Mullis, Chris Slagle, Ph.D., and Keri Hamilton, Ph.D. for writing portions of the manuscript as well as Whitman Bolles, Jessica Lerch, Ph.D., and Erin Kaltenbrun, Ph.D. for their careful review of the book.

We have all worked on this manuscript outside of the regular responsibilities of our careers, and this has only been possible with the supportive understanding of our families. We thank them for their patience as we worked late into the night to meet our deadlines.

Finally, we thank <u>you</u>, the reader and entrepreneur, for your dedication and commitment to advancing new scientific breakthroughs that are the reason the NIH SBIR/STTR program exists, and why it is so successful.

Winning SBIR/STTR Grants:
A Twelve-Week Plan for Preparing Your NIH Phase II Application

Section I - Commercialization Plan

Objectives

In contrast to your Phase I SBIR/STTR application, in which only a brief discussion of your technology's commercial potential is required, the Phase II application includes a comprehensive commercialization strategy detailed in your 12-page Commercialization Plan.

This Section guides you through a 12-week process in which you will review all of the required components of the Commercialization Plan, start working immediately on those tasks with long lead times, and write your full Commercialization Plan. The time required for each of these activities will depend on how much material you already have available from your business plan and other corporate documents and will usually range from 50 to 100 hours.

Tasks

1. Review the requirements of the Commercialization Plan and initiate tasks with long lead times. (*Week 1*)

2. Conduct market research. (*Weeks 2-4*)

3. Write your Commercialization Plan. (*Weeks 5-8*)

4. Obtain feedback from experts. (*Weeks 9-10*)

5. Complete the final draft of your Commercialization Plan. (*Week 11*)

Section I - Commercialization Plan

1. Review the requirements of the Commercialization Plan and initiate tasks with long lead times. (*Week 1*)

The Commercialization Plan consists of seven sections, which are defined in the Application Guide. The following Table provides a high-level overview of the objective of each of these sections:

Component	Objective
Value of SBIR/STTR Project, Expected Outcomes, and Impact	Provide a high-level overview of the relevance of your project to human health and to society in general
Company	Demonstrate that you have assembled an expert team capable of successfully commercializing your product
Market, Customer, and Competition	Establish your product's commercial relevance: its beneficiaries, its target users, and its advantages over current standards
Intellectual Property (IP) Protection	Describe your current IP portfolio and plan to maintain a competitive advantage by building a strong patent portfolio, protecting trade secrets, or other means
Finance Plan	Outline your strategy to fund future development and commercialization of your product beyond SBIR Phase II activities
Production and Marketing Plan	Describe how you will manufacture your product as well as your marketing strategy to reach your target customer
Revenue Stream	Explain how you will profit from your product's commercialization and how you will adapt to the market's evolving needs

During your first week of preparing your Commercialization Plan, you should develop an understanding of what materials will be required to complete each of the required sections. Then, you can initiate tasks with the longest lead times, including

Section I - Commercialization Plan

contacting individuals for Letters of Support and developing your financial plan.

\>\> Familiarize yourself with the contents of the Commercialization Plan.

- Read the description of the Commercialization Plan in the "SBIR/STTR Information Form" section of the Application Guide. The guidelines for this section are approximately 2 pages long.

- Some NIH Institutes, such as the National Institute of Allergy and Infectious Diseases (NIAID), publish sample Phase II applications on their websites. Obtain at least one of these sample applications, ideally for a technology that is similar to yours, so that you can read a successful Commercialization Plan.

\>\> Review the formatting requirements.

- The Application Guide provides very detailed instructions about font size, margins, line spacing, and even type density! Review these guidelines, and make sure you are maximizing your available space (such as utilizing 0.5" margins) and that you are adhering to the guidelines.

- The allowable length of the Commercialization Plan is 12 pages. You may choose either to include references within the 12 pages or to list them in the "References" section of the proposal. We recommend including the references within the

Section I - Commercialization Plan

12-page plan if you have space available, so that it is easier for reviewers to locate them.

>> Identify and contact individuals who will provide Letters of Support.

☐ For your Phase II proposal, it is very important to include approximately 4-5 Letters of Support from experts validating the commercial potential of your technology. Individuals who you may consider contacting to provide the letters include:

- Potential end-users (doctors, patient advocacy groups)

- Key opinion leaders (experts in the field)

- Investors (angels, venture capitalists)

- Leaders at potential partnering organizations (pharmaceutical companies, etc.)

☐ There are several effective strategies for making connections with potential partners and investors who may be willing to write Letters of Support. You can often meet key individuals at scientific or investment conferences. You can reach out by phone or in person to private foundations, patient advocacy groups, physicians, and other key opinion leaders. Additionally, you can ask your existing connections for contacts. For example, you may have a strategic investor who can connect you with experts in the field.

Section I - Commercialization Plan

☐ Once a connection has been made, set up an introductory meeting. Describe your product and your commercial value proposition. Explain your strategy for seeking non-dilutive funding and what will be accomplished under the Phase II grant award. Offer to share additional information, such as your Specific Aims or business plan. Then, ask for the individual's feedback and listen carefully to any advice they provide. If you are uncomfortable requesting a Letter of Support during this introductory meeting, you may wait to ask for a letter until after your new contact has a chance to learn more about your technology. Always thank the contacts for their advice and opinion, even if it is not what you wanted to hear! The process of reaching out to key individuals for Letters of Support has the added benefit of ensuring your technology is truly of interest to key stakeholders, which will be critical for you to successfully commercialize your product.

☐ Once your contact has agreed to provide a Letter of Support, offer to provide the individual with a draft letter to edit and sign. A strong letter will be approximately one page in length, and will include:

> **Helpful Hint**
>
> Request Letters of Support from individuals at companies early – some companies require legal approval before releasing Letters of Support.

1. The problem that your technology will address.

2. How your technology is distinct from other solutions.

Section I - Commercialization Plan

3. A brief bio of the letter writer to confirm that the individual has the appropriate expertise to evaluate your technology.

4. The specific interest the letter writer has in your technology. For example, a clinician can discuss impact on patients; an investor can discuss potential investment return.

5. A commitment from the letter writer to help support your technology development. Possible commitments can include a willingness to provide strategic advice as you advance through Phase II, consideration of investing/partnering, support for a clinical trial, or another form of commitment in which the letter writer demonstrates a vested interest in your technology development.

It is a good idea to request Letters of Support from several potential partners and investors, as it is unfortunately common for anticipated letters to fall through. There is no limit on the number of letters that you can provide, so if you are very successful in obtaining multiple letters, they can all be included in the application.

>> Identify and contact individuals who can assist with preparing the financial information for your Commercialization Plan. You are required to include: a) your history of funding; b) a breakdown of funds needed for commercializing your product; c) the anticipated sources of this funding; and d) revenue projections for post-market entry. Unless you have a background

Section I - Commercialization Plan

in finance, you will likely need to identify third parties to assist with this requirement.

- ☐ If you have a Chief Financial Officer (CFO), this individual should be able to assist you with obtaining the information you will need for the proposal.

- ☐ If you do not have a CFO (which is a common scenario for small, early-stage companies applying for their first Phase II SBIR/STTR), you can reach out to other resources for support, such as small business development centers (SBDCs) or consultants with expertise in developing business plans and Commercialization Plans.

- ☐ Once you have identified individuals who can assist you with developing the financial portions of your Commercialization Plan, request specific information that you need for sections **e. Finance Plan, f. Production and Marketing Plan**, and **g. Revenue Stream** (see below). Be sure to provide a deadline for the delivery of these items. It may be helpful to provide these individuals with examples of funded Commercialization Plans from the sample SBIRs that you reviewed earlier in this Task.

At the end of this first week, you should have a good understanding of the requirements for a strong Commercialization Plan, and your long lead-time items should be well underway! You are now ready to focus on conducting market research so as to establish the commercial need for your product.

Section I - Commercialization Plan

2. Conduct market research. (*Weeks 2-4*)

Your Commercialization Plan must provide a clear picture of the current and future market opportunity for your technology. We suggest you devote a 3-week period completely to market research, given how important this information will be for a successful submission. The first week should be spent identifying resources, and then you can spend two full weeks extracting the information that you need from these resources. During this 3-week period, remember to check on the tasks with long lead times that you started in Week 1, to ensure they remain on track.

>> Identify reference sources to support the unmet need and commercial opportunity for your technology.

☐ Peer-reviewed scientific publications may include statistics on the prevalence, associated morbidity, and economic burden. Review articles can be particularly good sources for this information.

☐ Government and private sources (such as foundations) often publish pamphlets providing market information.

☐ The NIH Institute that funded your Phase I proposal may provide up-to-date information about the unmet need that you are addressing, as well as any new breakthroughs, on its website.

☐ Several programs offer market assessments for your product. For example, the NIH Niche Assessment Program (NAP) provides valuable feedback from potential customers

Section I - Commercialization Plan

and may help direct your commercialization approach. Other programs may be available at local incubators or business centers.

\>\> Obtain relevant market reports.

☐ Market reports focusing on specific technology sectors can be purchased online; however, they can be cost-prohibitive for small businesses. Check with your local libraries or university libraries for market report availability. Additionally, many online market reports have portions that are viewable without purchase. Occasionally, you can contact the market report publisher to request a free sample chapter that may contain relevant information for your proposal.

☐ Image-search results can be helpful for finding charts and figures on market size, growth, and market share. You can use these charts or figures in your Commercialization Plan (with appropriate citations) to effectively summarize the target market.

☐ Even if you find a single market research report that provides you with most or all of the relevant market data that you need for your Commercialization Plan, it is best to cite a minimum of 1-2 additional primary sources, such as scientific publications or government reports.

\>\> Identify relevant information from source materials to include in the Commercialization Plan.

Section I - Commercialization Plan

☐ Key information to note includes:

- Target-addressable market size, both U.S. and global

- Projected growth

- Market segments

- Current market leaders

- Market drivers

- Barriers to market entry

- Potential competitors and new technologies

☐ Include well-supported numbers whenever possible. It is especially effective to include data on the number of people directly and indirectly affected by the problem that you are solving, as well as associated financial cost. Include both current and projected numbers.

> *Helpful Hint*
>
> *Your Commercialization Plan should define both the total market and addressable market. For example, the total market may be all patients with a specific disease, but the addressable market is the subset of the patients that you expect will benefit from your final commercialized product.*

By the end of Task 3, you will have collected comprehensive data about the market that you are targeting, including market drivers, as well as current and future competitive technologies. In

Section I - Commercialization Plan

the next Task, you will use this information to write your Commercialization Plan.

3. Write your Commercialization Plan. *(Weeks 5-8)*

The Commercialization Plan consists of the following sections:

a. Value of the SBIR/STTR Project, Expected Outcomes, and Impact
b. Company
c. Market, Customer, and Competition
d. Intellectual Property Protection
e. Finance Plan
f. Production and Marketing Plan
g. Revenue Stream

We strongly recommend that you format your Commercialization Plan in exactly this order, listing each section as a heading. Keeping to this format will assist reviewers in finding the information they need to provide a fair critique.

As you write each section, keep in mind that the overarching objective of the Commercialization Plan is to impress upon reviewers that your product has a viable and well-planned route to commercialization, that it will uniquely address a significant unmet need, and that your company has the necessary expertise to support product development and commercialization. This is accomplished by presenting a clear, logical value proposition, development plan, and financial strategy.

Before you start writing, read the instructions for each section of the Commercialization Plan in the Application Guide to ensure you are addressing all requirements. The guidelines below are

Section I - Commercialization Plan

intended to supplement, not replace, the instructions in the Application Guide.

a. Value of the SBIR/STTR Project, Expected Outcomes, and Impact (1-2 pages)

>> Begin your Commercialization Plan with the section header "**a. Value of the SBIR/STTR Project, Expected Outcomes, and Impact.**"

>> Consider using the three section topics (*Value of the Project, Expected Outcomes, and Impact*) as separate subheaders. Alternatively, you may customize your subheaders to emphasize key points such as *Value Proposition, Unmet Need, [Name of Disease]*, etc.

>> Discuss the *Value of the SBIR/STTR Project.*

☐ Summarize concisely the scope of your project, in layperson's terms. It may seem redundant to provide a summary of your project here, since you include similar summaries in several other sections of the proposal. However, this is an important opportunity to set the stage for the business value proposition of your product. Provide a summary that incorporates a more business-oriented tone rather than the scientific-oriented style that you will use throughout the rest of the application.

> *Helpful Hint*
>
> *If you have a professional image depicting your technology from your website or marketing material, this is a good place to include it.*

Section I - Commercialization Plan

☐ Describe the <u>unmet health need</u> that your product will specifically address. For example, in the case of a disease, describe quantitatively the morbidity and mortality that is associated with the disease. You may include more statistics related to incidence, impact, and costs (graphs, charts, etc.) in this section than you will be able to fit in the Significance section of your Research Plan.

☐ Provide an overview of the <u>economic market</u> that you will address. You will provide more detail on this in later sections, but here you should state the economic opportunity associated with your addressable market. Also, define whether you will be entering an existing market or if you anticipate a new market for your technology.

>> Describe the *Expected Outcomes*.

☐ Approach this subsection by painting a picture of the "before" and "after" scenarios of your technology being commercialized. For example, the "before" may describe handwritten doctors' notes that are subject to errors while the "after" is a completely digital medical report that will reduce errors by 99% and allow for integration with a patient's full medical record. A common mistake is for applicants to assume that the outcomes associated with commercialization of their technologies will be obvious to reviewers. It is your responsibility to clearly demonstrate to reviewers the immediate and long-term outcomes that your product will facilitate.

Section I - Commercialization Plan

\>\> Define the *Impact*.

> ☐ Describe the impact that your project will have on several areas of society, including health benefits, economic benefits, educational benefits, and scientific advancement.
>
> ☐ Benchmark each impact against existing technologies to highlight how your technology provides an improvement over current standards.

\>\> Clearly restate the value proposition in your final paragraph of this section. Specifically, indicate <u>what</u> your project will accomplish, and <u>why</u> it is so important to fund your project. The remainder of the Commercialization Plan will cover <u>how</u> you will accomplish these objectives.

b. Company (1-2 pages)

\>\> Begin with the section header "**b. Company.**" Subheaders may include: *Origin of Company, Company Objectives, Core Competencies, Team,* and *History of Funding and Commercialization.*

\>\> Describe the *Company's Origins*.

> ☐ Include a brief history of your company and founders. This is a great opportunity to provide color and background as to how the technology was discovered and the motivation for the formation of the company.

Section I - Commercialization Plan

\>> Define the *Key Milestones*.

☐ Describe the achievements of the company to date. These may include technical milestones, business milestones, and hiring of key personnel. Use this section to demonstrate that your company has a history of achieving targeted milestones.

\>> Describe your *Team*.

☐ A description of your key personnel is arguably the most important part of the Company section, given that "Investigators" is a specific review criterion. Reviewers will evaluate whether you have gaps in scientific, clinical, regulatory, business, legal, and other expertise required to advance your technology to commercialization. If you don't have all of the necessary personnel lined up, it is helpful to list names and/or roles of the individuals who you plan to add to your team in the future.

> **Helpful Hint**
>
> *If your company is relatively young with no commercialization history, it is particularly important to include individuals on your team with a history of successfully commercializing new technologies.*

☐ Consider listing your team in table format, with the first column describing the type of expertise, the second column naming the individual and role, and the third column providing a few bullet points on the individual's background.

☐ Include all individuals who provide scientific and business expertise to the company. In addition to your key employees,

Section I - Commercialization Plan

include relevant consultants, academic collaborators, members of your Board of Directors, and members of your Scientific Advisory Board, if applicable.

>> State your *Funding History*.

☐ Provide a table indicating sources and amounts of funding (including grant, angel, and investor funding), as well as date received.

☐ Describe what milestones were accomplished with each round of funding to date to demonstrate your company's history of success.

☐ Some companies express concern that they have received either "too much" or "too little" prior funding to be competitive for a Phase II SBIR/STTR. However, companies ranging from having $0 in external funding to >$50M have secured Phase II SBIR/STTR grants. If your company has relatively little external funding to date, you will need to indicate how the current Phase II funding will enable you to obtain the data needed to motivate additional outside investment. If your company has already raised substantial funds, you will need to indicate why the Phase II funding will be important for advancing this specific project. For example, the Phase II funds may support development of a product that is considered too high-risk for current investors; however, completion of your Phase II aims will sufficiently de-risk the technology to motivate outside investment.

Section I - Commercialization Plan

\>\> Define your *Future Plans.*

☐ Provide an outlook of the long-term future for your company. Indicate which areas of core expertise you will continue to develop internally, and which tasks you will outsource.

☐ Describe your plans to partner/license your technology and/or to develop additional internal capabilities to support commercialization of your technology.

☐ List any projected future hires that would lead to job creation, which is an important metric for the success of the SBIR/STTR program.

☐ Describe your product pipeline and indicate how the current project will broadly support your future product development objectives.

> *Helpful Hint*
>
> *Your proposal will likely receive more favorable "Overall Impact" scores if you convey that the Phase II project will open the door for future products or services that are beyond the scope of the initial proposed product.*

c. Market, Customer, and Competition (3-4 pages)

\>\> Begin with the section header "**c. Market, Customer, and Competition.**" Each of these topics can also be used as subheaders.

Section I - Commercialization Plan

>> Define your *Market*.

☐ This section utilizes all the market information that you have worked so hard to obtain over the past several weeks! You will need to provide evidence that: 1) there is a significant market for your technology, and 2) that your technology has the ability to penetrate the market. It is effective to use graphs and charts in this subsection to clearly illustrate the market need. The following points should be addressed:

- Target Market: Describe the total size of your target market and any relevant market sub-segments based on information gathered from market reports and other references. Discuss projected growth of the market over the timeframe during which you will commercialize your product.

- Market Drivers: Define the external factors that influence the market. For example, if you are developing a product to address aging, the increasing elderly population and rising cost of healthcare may be market drivers that support a growing unmet need for your product. You should include not only information obtained from market reports, but also any information you have obtained by talking to potential customers, licensing partners, and experts in the field.

- Niche Markets: In some cases, a product may address a relatively small market but target a substantial unmet human health need. For example, you may be developing a novel therapeutic for an orphan disease. In the case of a

Section I - Commercialization Plan

small market, you need to have an especially well-developed plan for obtaining the financing you will need for commercialization, as it may be more challenging to attract investors who are looking for a large return on their investment.

• <u>Partnerships</u>: Forming relationships with partnering organizations can be an effective way to address any gaps you may have on your own team. For example, if you partner with a large company, you may not need to build your own manufacturing facility or sales force. However, you will need to provide credible evidence to reviewers that your target partners are interested in working with you by including Letters of Support from these potential partners.

• <u>Barriers to Commercialization</u>: Define the major hurdles that you will need to overcome to commercialize your product. These may include obtaining regulatory approval, scaling up production, recruiting for clinical trials, and/or securing a partnership. Identify approximately 2-4 hurdles as well as a detailed plan for how you will overcome each hurdle. Include viable, well-developed back-up plans for all potential barriers.

\>\> Define your *Customer*.

☐ Identify both the early adopters and the long-term customers for your product. Define your direct customer, as well as indirect customers. A direct customer may be a larger company or hospital system, while the indirect customer may be the patient who will benefit from the product.

Section I - Commercialization Plan

- Explain your strategy for accessing your targeted customers. There are many examples of excellent products that did not receive market traction, so you will need a well-developed plan for turning your "leads" into "customers." If using a partnership approach, highlight your partner's established customer base.

\>\> Describe your *Competition*.

- A common mistake is for applicants to discount their competition. Statements such as "we have no competitors" can derail your proposal, as <u>every product will have some competition</u>. Instead, present a very detailed profile of all other technologies that address the same unmet need as your technology. This provides you with an opportunity to clearly delineate the unique advantages of your approach.

- Consider creating a table that compares key features of your technology with those of your competitors. Include both current and potential future competitors who have products in development. Comparison criteria may include price point, stage of development, associated risks, benefits, side effects, and other criteria relevant to your market.

- Emphasize how your technology will address limitations of current products.

\>\> Given the importance of the **Market, Customer, and Competition** section, carefully review this section to ensure that you have thoroughly addressed the following key review criteria:

Section I - Commercialization Plan

- ☐ Clearly defined market opportunity.

- ☐ Plans for engaging your target customer.

- ☐ Strategies to address expected and unexpected hurdles.

- ☐ Differentiation from competitors.

d. IP Protection (0.5 pages)

>> Begin with the section header "**d. Intellectual Property (IP) Protection.**" You likely do not need to use subheaders for this section.

>> Describe how you will obtain and maintain a competitive advantage. In most cases, companies will seek IP protection through patents. However, in some businesses (notably, software), you may rely more heavily on trade secrets.

>> Include the name and background of your IP attorney.

>> Provide a list of all patent applications that your company has applied for directly and/or licensed.

- ☐ Include a short description of the coverage that each patent application provides.

- ☐ Indicate the prosecution status for each filing, and your strategy for seeking U.S. and/or international coverage.

Section I - Commercialization Plan

    ☐ If you are licensing IP that is held by a university, and you have a licensing agreement that gives the company rights to develop the technology, consider asking the university for a Letter of Support detailing this arrangement.

>> Describe the results of any Freedom to Operate (FTO) searches, if they have been conducted. If you have not had a formal FTO search, then explain why it is unlikely that competitors would be able to block you from developing the product that you are proposing.

>> State whether you intend to file additional patents either during or after the Phase II project period. If you currently have a patent portfolio that could be perceived as weak, it can be advantageous to state that you will apply for patent protection once key Phase II milestones are achieved.

e. Finance Plan (1 page)

>> Begin with the section header "**e. Finance Plan**." Subheaders for this section are not usually necessary.

>> Define the costs associated with each milestone you will need to meet to commercialize your technology. Then, explain your funding strategy to achieve each of these milestones.

    ☐ Remember that the SBIR/STTR program is officially a "3-phase" program. In Phases I and II, you receive grant funding from the government to assist you in overcoming technical hurdles to make your technology more attractive for third-

Section I - Commercialization Plan

party funding. In Phase III, you are expected to obtain non-grant funding to advance your product to commercialization.

☐ One possible strategy is to utilize grant funding to achieve scientific milestones and equity/partner funding to reach business and commercial milestones. Tapping into multiple sources of funding helps to de-risk your development and is generally viewed favorably by reviewers.

☐ Request *pro forma* financial projections from your CFO. It is effective to present these in table form or as a Gantt chart. Samples of both formats are provided on the following page. Note that many of the numbers will rely on an educated guess, but they should be reasonable projections in-line with other products that have been developed in your industry.

Section I - Commercialization Plan

Sample formats of pro forma financials

Year	2019	2020	2021	2022	2023	2024-2025
Milestone	Pre-IND studies		Phase 1 Clinical Trial	Phase 2 Clinical Trial		Phase 3 Clinical Trial, file NDA
Expenses						
IND-Enabling Studies	$700,000	$700,000				
CMC & GMP Manufacturing		$1,500,000				
Clinical Trials			$1,000,000	$2,250,000	$2,250,000	$10,000,000
Overhead	$300,000	$300,000	$500,000	$600,000	$600,000	$800,000
TOTAL	$1,000,000	$2,500,000	$1,500,000	$2,850,000	$2,850,000	$10,800,000
Revenue						
SBIR Phase II	$1,000,000	$1,000,000				
Series A		$1,500,000	$1,500,000			
Series B				$3,000,000	$3,000,000	
License or IPO						Licensing partner or IPO
TOTAL	$1,000,000	$2,500,000	$1,500,000	$3,000,000	$3,000,000	-
Funds at Y/E	0	0	0	$150,000	$300,000	-

	Pre-IND Studies		Phase 1 Clinical Trial	Phase 2 Clinical Trial		Phase 3 Clinical Trial; File NDA
	2019	2020	2021	2022	2023	2024-2025
IND-Enabling Studies	$1,400,000					
GMP Manufacturing		$1,500,000				
Clinical Trials			$1,000,000	$4,500,000		$10,000,000
Overhead	$300,000	$300,000	$500,000	$600,000	$600,000	$800,000
Funding sources	SBIR Phase II ($2M)		Series A ($3M)	Series B ($6M)		Partner / IPO

>> Letters of Support from potential investors or licensing partners can add credibility that you will be able to successfully secure financing for beyond Phase II. If you have already reached out to these sources for Letters of Support, this is a good time to check in with them. If you are struggling with obtaining solid funding commitments, a softer letter indicating interest in your technology and a willingness to evaluate the investment opportunity after you complete your Phase II milestones can still be helpful.

Section I - Commercialization Plan

f. Production and Marketing Plan (0.5 - 1 page)

\>> Begin with the section header "**f. Production and Marketing Plan.**" Each of these topics may also be used as a subheader.

\>> Describe your *Production* plans.

☐ If you will directly manufacture your product or if you will directly oversee the manufacturing, include a discussion of the following:

- Capability to produce the product
- Ability to achieve price-point
- Reproducibility and reliability
- Safety
- Plans to ensure supply will keep up with demand

☐ In the case of outsourcing production, provide names of potential contract manufacturers and estimated costs.

☐ Address special requirements for your product, such as Current Good Laboratory Practice (cGLP) and Current Good Manufacturing Practice (cGMP) standards.

☐ If you plan to partner with a larger company that will assume control of manufacturing, describe the capabilities and track record of the potential partner(s) in producing similar products.

>> Describe your *Marketing* plans.

☐ If your business strategy is to partner with a larger, more experienced company, the production and marketing will likely be handled by the partner company. Emphasize that the experience, reputation, and current customer base of the partner will be advantageous to commercial success.

☐ If you plan to cover the marketing internally, describe your existing sales and marketing expertise as well as your growth plans in these areas.

☐ Consider how you will reach out to key customers and what marketing techniques you expect will be most effective. In many cases, you can indicate that the SBIR/STTR Phase II data will be valuable in helping to convince potential customers of the benefits of your technology.

g. Revenue Stream (0.5 - 1 page)

>> Begin this final section with the header "**g. Revenue Stream.**" You do not need subheaders.

>> Provide a profit & loss (P&L) analysis for the first five years post-commercialization. Describe any assumptions that you have made in your analysis as well as any key risk factors in achieving your projected revenue (product adoption, changing market conditions, etc.).

Section I - Commercialization Plan

>> Describe any projected staffing changes post-commercialization. Include associated costs in your financial projections.

>> Indicate whether any of your profits will be used to fund additional R&D to support a future pipeline of products and company sustainability.

4. Obtain feedback from experts. (*Weeks 9-10*)

Once you have completed the first draft of your Commercialization Plan, feedback from neutral third parties can be invaluable for identifying and addressing gaps in your Commercialization Plan. Allow at least 2 weeks turnaround for reviewers to provide you with their critiques.

>> Choose 2-3 experts to review your Commercialization Plan with a fresh, objective approach. Identify an SBIR/STTR expert, a business development expert, and/or a domain subject expert.

>> Ask your reviewers to evaluate how well your Commercialization Plan addresses the following review criteria:

- Will the proposed studies contribute significantly to the commercial viability of the envisioned final product?

- Will commercialization of the technology have a meaningful societal impact?

- Does the company demonstrate prior achievement of R&D and business milestones?

Section I - Commercialization Plan

- Is the company's team qualified and capable of completing commercialization of the technology?

- Will the work funded in Phase II generate external investment interest?

- Does the company demonstrate a clear grasp of the relevant commercial market and a logical strategy for market penetration?

- Has the company developed a practical, long-term vision for revenue generation following commercialization of their technology?

\>\> Arrange for a follow-up meeting or phone call with your reviewers to discuss their critiques. If they are willing to review additional drafts, it can be helpful to obtain their feedback on whether you successfully addressed their concerns.

5. Complete the final draft of your Commercialization Plan. (*Week 11*)

At this point, you may feel like you never want to look at your Commercialization Plan again! However, dedicating a few hours to a comprehensive final review can proactively address potential reviewer critiques and provide you with a highly polished final product that transforms your proposal from "good" to "excellent."

\>\> Incorporate the feedback that you received from experts. If you don't agree with any of the feedback that you have received, keep in mind that the Study Section reviewers are likely to have

Section I - Commercialization Plan

similar reactions to your proposal as your expert reviewers. Therefore, it is a good idea to carefully consider all reviewer feedback and to modify your proposal to proactively address any anticipated reviewer questions or concerns.

>> Carefully review your Commercialization Plan for correct grammar and formatting. Some investigators may argue that grammar and proposal structure are not relevant as long as the scientific and business value propositions are compelling. However, reviewers may feel that poor grammar represents a lack of dedication and commitment and will therefore be more likely to give better scores to proposals that are polished. Additionally, a well-written proposal is easier for reviewers to read, ensuring that your message is clearly received. If you don't have the internal expertise to carefully proof-read the Commercialization Plan, it is worthwhile to engage an external editor. This is money well-spent, considering that careful proofreading can make the difference in receiving millions of dollars of funding for your company.

If you are a scientist, writing a Commercialization Plan may have been a particularly challenging task. Congratulations on achieving this milestone! You will likely be eager to move on to the next section of this book, the Research Plan, which is probably much more in your comfort zone.

Section II - Research Plan

Objectives

The Phase II **Research Plan** consists of a **Specific Aims** page, followed by your **Research Strategy**. The two main differences between the Phase I and Phase II Research Strategy sections are:

1) The length of the Research Strategy can be up to 12 pages in Phase II, compared to the 6-page limit in Phase I.

2) A Progress Report summarizing your results from Phase I is included in the 12-page Phase II Research Strategy.

In this Section, you will first develop your Phase II scope of work, and then prepare each section of the Research Plan. Approximately 100 hours will be required to finish these tasks.

Tasks

1. Define the scope of your Phase II project and initiate long lead-time items. (*Week 1*)

2. Perform a current literature search. (*Week 2*)

3. Write the Specific Aims page. (*Week 3*)

4. Prepare the first draft of your Research Strategy. (*Weeks 4-8*)

5. Obtain feedback from experts. (*Weeks 9-10*)

6. Complete the final draft of your Research Plan. (*Week 11*)

Section II - Research Plan

1. Define the scope of your Phase II project and initiate long lead-time items. (*Week 1*)

Chances are that the NIH has updated the Application Guide since your Phase I submission. It is therefore useful to re-familiarize yourself with the Research Plan instructions. You should then define the scope of work for your Phase II project and start working on long lead-time items, such as obtaining quotes from CROs and budgets from subcontractors.

>> Read the entire instructions for the Research Plan in the PHS 398 Research Plan Form in the Application Guide. Pay close attention to new requirements that have been added since your Phase I submission. If you are uncertain about the instructions for specific sections, contact your Program Officer as early as possible in the process to request clarification.

>> Review other funded Phase II proposals to obtain examples of the scope of work in successfully funded applications.

- Search the "NIH RePORTER" website for projects with activity codes R44 (SBIR Phase II) and R42 (STTR Phase II) and key words relevant to your project.

- Review the abstracts of the funded proposals, and make note of the projects' scope of work.

- Pay particular attention to proposals that are funded by the same NIH Institute/Center (IC) as your Phase I project. The types of projects that are funded, as well as the overall budget, can vary greatly among the ICs.

Section II - Research Plan

>> Review the Summary Statement from your Phase I proposal, and be sure to proactively address any concerns or gaps identified by your Phase I reviewers as you assemble your Phase II Research Plan.

>> Develop your plan of work for your Phase II project.

☐ The purpose of your Phase I project was to de-risk your technology through proof-of-concept work. Your proposed Phase II studies should be less risky than your Phase I studies and should move your technology toward commercialization.

> *Helpful Hint*
>
> *Your Phase II studies should be the "Development" component of your "R&D" activities. In Phase I, you conducted **research** to assess your product's feasibility. In Phase II, you should **develop** your product for its intended commercial market.*

• Avoid proposing basic research in your Phase II proposal. This is a common mistake, especially for investigators who are used to preparing R01 applications.

• Think of Phase II as a vertical progression toward a product rather than a horizontal expansion of the fundamental innovation into additional areas. For example, if you have shown efficacy toward a particular type of cancer in Phase I, it is better to move the product vertically toward commercialization for that cancer type in Phase II rather than expanding to new cancer types.

Section II - Research Plan

- Clearly define your "target product profile" (TPP), and use your Phase II project to advance as efficiently as possible toward the TPP.

☐ Defining the scope of your Phase II project is likely the most important decision you will make during the entire proposal preparation process, so make sure you utilize all available resources to guide this important decision. Resources may include internal scientific experts, CROs, subcontractors, outside consultants, and your PO.

☐ Once you define your Phase II project scope, you are ready to hit the ground running in preparing a strong Research Plan. You should consider this stage of defining your Phase II objectives similar to a "design freeze" – once you decide on your Phase II scope of work, don't change it! If you keep switching around your Phase II plan as you prepare your proposal, it will be extremely difficult to prepare a competitive application.

>> Initiate long lead-time items.

☐ Establish relationships with and request quotes from CROs/subcontractors and subawardees who will conduct portions of the proposed work.

- Clearly communicate the relevant scope of work to these entities.

- For subawardees at academic institutions, reach out to the institute's pre-award office. Academic institutions will likely require a significant amount of time for internal review and preparation of documents you will need for the submission of your application.

☐ Contact consultants who can fill gaps in your company's internal expertise.

• Identify the consultant's expertise and how it fits into your Phase II project.

• Once a consultant has agreed to support your project, request their curriculum vitae and adapt it to the NIH Biographical Sketch format.

• Consultant Letters of Support should include hourly rates and the estimated time commitment during the course of the project.

2. Perform a current literature search. (*Week 2*)

A significant amount of time has passed since the preparation of your Phase I application, and new publications relevant to your technology have likely been released. As an entrepreneur developing a cutting-edge product, it is extremely important to convey to reviewers that you are up to date with your field.

>> Update your list of references to support your Significance and Innovation sections.

Section II - Research Plan

☐ Conduct a "cited reference search" to obtain a list of publications that have referenced any of the key literature that you cited in your Phase I application.

☐ Review the most recent Study Section roster of the SRG to which you are planning to submit your proposal. Identify any members who are leaders in your field, and make sure you cite any key work that they have contributed.

☐ Search for any new publications released by leaders in the field.

☐ Search meeting abstracts, patent applications, and market reports for additional cutting edge research related to your field.

As you review the new literature, keep in mind ways that you can differentiate your technology from other state-of-the-art work in your field.

3. Write the Specific Aims page. (*Week 3*)

\>> Begin this 1-page section with the header "**Specific Aims**."

\>> In the first paragraph, provide a brief summary of the unmet need that your technology will address, including the healthcare, financial, and societal burdens.

\>> In the second paragraph, introduce your company's technology. Provide an overview of how your technology addresses the unmet need, and the progress that you have made

Section II - Research Plan

so far (including during your Phase I project period) in advancing your product toward commercialization.

\>\> In the third paragraph, describe the next stage(s) of development required to bring your technology to commercialization, and discuss how your planned Phase II project will accomplish these goals. End this paragraph with a sentence that segues into your proposal's Specific Aims.

\>\> List the Specific Aims of your Phase II proposal. For each Aim, provide a very brief statement of the experimental approach, the metrics you will use to determine success of the studies, and the developmental milestones that will be achieved by successfully completing each Aim.

\>\> Conclude the Specific Aims page with the anticipated final outcome of your Phase II project (e.g., submission of an IND application to the FDA). Briefly describe the long-term goals for your product, including its impact on the unmet need it addresses.

4. Prepare the first draft of your Research Strategy (*Weeks 4-8*)

The three sections of the Phase II Research Strategy (Significance, Innovation, and Approach) are the same as for Phase I. Since you have 6 additional pages compared to Phase I, you can further develop key points in each of these sections. Your Phase II Research Strategy should provide a strong scientific premise for your proposed Phase II activities and should follow logically from your Phase I results.

Section II - Research Plan

a. Significance (1 page)

\>\> Begin with the section header "**Significance**."

\>\> Clearly define the unmet need.

□ This section provides an opportunity to paint the "before" picture of the world without your technology. Make sure the unmet need is sufficiently developed so reviewers recognize that there is a clear and real need, and that no current solutions adequately address this need.

□ Similar to your Phase I proposal, you should be as specific as possible in defining the unmet need that your product will address. You have likely narrowed down a target market since submission of your Phase I application, and you should focus on the specific population who will benefit from your product.

□ Describe all recent advances in the field. Include information from the literature search that you conducted in Week 2.

\>\> Define the **Scientific Premise**.

□ Scientific Premise is a review criterion in which the committee evaluates whether the applicant has sufficiently discussed the strengths and weaknesses of prior research that supports the current application. The strength or weakness of the Scientific Premise will be reflected in the "Significance" and "Overall Impact" scores.

Section II - Research Plan

☐ Identify the progression of prior research (your own and other groups' work) that led to the basis of your proposed work. Evaluate the validity of this prior research, including strengths and weaknesses of the experimental approaches, the analytical methods, and the conclusions drawn from these studies.

☐ Discuss the ways in which your Phase I results further support the scientific foundation for your Phase II proposal.

☐ Define how your Phase II program will fill a gap in scientific knowledge.

b. Innovation (1 page)

\>\> Begin with the section header "**Innovation**."

\>\> Explain how your technology's innovation will uniquely address the unmet need defined in the Significance section.

☐ Start with a description of the differentiators that your product provides over other solutions.

☐ Describe the specific impact on the field that will result from your technology development.

☐ Explain why your company/team is uniquely positioned to develop the technology.

☐ For an SBIR/STTR proposal, it is not critical that your technology be paradigm-changing in the field (such as discovery of a new biological pathway). However, if your innovation does have paradigm-changing potential, make sure you state this.

☐ Discuss broader impacts of your technology. Although you are currently applying your innovation to a specific problem, you can also state longer-term impacts of your technology. For example, you may be proposing to develop an innovative new treatment for bacterial infections. Though your Phase II proposal's scope of work should focus on one particular indication, point out in the Innovation section that your product may ultimately be applicable to multiple indications.

c. Approach (~9 pages)

Your Approach will include a Progress Report summarizing your Phase I results, followed by your plan of work for Phase II. Reviewers will analyze the quality of your Phase I data to evaluate the likelihood that you will be able to successfully execute your proposed Phase II studies. High-quality data along with appropriate use of controls and statistical analysis in Phase I will increase reviewers' confidence in your ability to carry out the Phase II project.

\>\> Before writing your Approach section, take the time to review the *NIH Requirements for Rigor, Reproducibility, and Transparency*. These guidelines are intended to enhance reproducibility of research findings through increased scientific rigor and transparency and should be followed in your experimental design.

Section II - Research Plan

\>> Begin with the section header "**Approach**."

\>> Add a subsection header "**Progress Report**," and indicate the dates of the Phase I project period.

\>> Provide a brief overview of the overall objective of the Phase I program, and the proof-of-concept experiment(s) that you proposed.

- Reviewers will typically have access to your Phase I Summary Statement, which includes the Project Summary, but will not have access to the full Phase I proposal. However, it is common for your Phase I reviewers to also be assigned to review your Phase II application, so they may remember the full scope of work proposed in your Phase I project.

\>> Report the results that you obtained for each of your Phase I Specific Aims.

- Under the heading for each Aim, write a brief paragraph that summarizes the overall purpose of the Aim.

- Describe the studies that were performed, the results, and your conclusions.

> *Helpful Hint*
>
> *Your Phase I Progress Report should read similarly to a research publication. Include a similar level of detail as you would for submission to a peer-reviewed journal.*

- Provide a comprehensive statistical analysis.

- Include graphs and tables to concisely present data.

Section II - Research Plan

- If you modified your Phase I project substantially from what you originally proposed, you should carefully evaluate your data to determine if you are ready to advance to Phase II. If you modified your planned studies but achieved the same stated Phase I milestones, you can explain the modifications in the Progress Report to justify advancement to Phase II. However, if your project failed to demonstrate feasibility, your research program is not ready for Phase II. In this case, it is best to use the lessons you have learned during your first Phase I program to re-design your studies and submit a new Phase I application that can successfully demonstrate feasibility.

>> Present any additional supporting data gathered outside of your Phase I program. During the course of the Phase I project period, you may have conducted additional studies that further support advancement to Phase II, and these can be described in your Progress Report.

>> Clearly indicate how the results of your Phase I project justify further development of your technology.

>> Add a subheader, such as **"Phase II Studies,"** to transition from the Phase I Progress Report to your Phase II proposed scope of work.

>> Write the experimental approach in support of your Phase II Aims.

- For each Aim/Sub-aim, describe the purpose of the experiment(s) and the methodology you will employ, including references for all aspects of your experimental

Section II - Research Plan

protocol that are based on literature precedence. If you are proposing new methodologies, you should provide solid rationale for their scientific validity and technical feasibility.

☐ Describe the statistical analysis that you will employ. Support your proposed sample size and number of replicates, referencing your Phase I data as applicable.

> **Helpful Hint**
>
> *Make sure key points in your Approach stand out for reviewers through the use of bold, italics, and/or underlining. Consider creating separate sections for Alternative Approaches and Metrics of Success so that they are easily identifiable.*

☐ For each Aim/Sub-aim, include an "Alternative Approaches" paragraph that describes problems that could arise and steps that you will take to address them.

☐ Include a "Metrics of Success" section for each Aim/Sub-aim. Describe precisely the metrics that must be achieved for the experiment to be considered successful and how this will advance your technology toward commercialization. The metrics of success should be quantitative and measurable so that the reviewers have a clear picture of what a go/no-go result will look like.

>> Ensure your plan of work takes into account each of the following NIH requirements:

☐ *A strong, clearly-stated scientific premise*. Refer to the data in your Phase I Progress Report to establish a sound scientific basis for the development work you propose in Phase II.

Section II - Research Plan

☐ *Lack of bias.* Your Research Strategy should include consideration of the strengths and limitations of published research and your Progress Report data. Similarly, for each new study you propose in your Research Strategy, you should describe not only the anticipated outcome, but also any limitations or pitfalls you are likely to encounter and alternative strategies that could overcome these pitfalls. Expert reviewers are likely to know the limitations of your technology, so it is best to address these limitations directly.

☐ *Robust study designs.* When designing your studies, you should demonstrate that the sample sizes for your studies are large enough to ensure adequate statistical power and provide an explanation of how these sample sizes were chosen. Also incorporate the appropriate control groups, conditions, and reagents so that your experimental results cannot be attributed to chance, artifacts, or other circumstances. Studies using human subjects and vertebrate animals must consider all relevant biological variables, such as sex, that may influence the results. Make sure you have included appropriate methods for randomization and blinding. Incorporate appropriate statistical analysis methods to correctly determine significance of the parameters you are measuring.

>> Include a timeline, which may be presented in the form of a Gantt chart or a table, so that reviewers can visualize how you plan to schedule your experiments throughout the grant period.

>> Write a conclusion paragraph that emphasizes the importance and relevance of your Phase II work. The conclusion to your

Section II - Research Plan

Approach section is your last chance to convince reviewers that they should fund your proposal!

>> Carefully review your Approach and ensure it addresses all points in the "Research Project Evaluation Criteria" in the "Peer Review Process" section of the Application Guide.

5. Obtain feedback from experts (*Weeks 9-10*)

>> Identify 2-3 experts to review your Research Plan. Ask them to evaluate your draft for each of the following NIH review criteria:

- A clearly-stated scientific premise that forms the basis for the proposed research. For a Phase II project, the proof-of-concept data obtained during your Phase I work should strongly support your scientific premise.

- An unbiased discussion of the scientific literature relevant to your technology and an unbiased review of your competition.

- Clearly stated rationale for the experimental design of your Specific Aims and up-to-date literature citations to support the experimental methods.

- Rationales for the particular animal strains/species chosen for any animal work, and a discussion of other biological variables such as animal age, sex, and weight that may influence results.

Section II - Research Plan

☐ A plan for statistical treatment of data that describes the reasoning behind the choice of sample size for each experiment and an explanation of controls for each experiment.

☐ Thoughtful consideration of any limitations of the proposed studies and a discussion of possible strategies to overcome these limitations.

6. Complete the final draft of your Research Plan. (*Week 11*)

\>\> Incorporate feedback from your solicited experts and write your final Research Plan.

\>\> Conduct a final check for correct grammar and formatting.

Congratulations, you have completed your Research Plan!

Section III- Other Components

Objectives

Sections I and II covered preparation of the Commercialization Plan and Research Plan, as these documents are the heart of your proposal. However, these two components represent only 25 pages of your approximately 150-200 page Phase II submission. The remaining components will supplement your Commercialization and Research Plans with additional details and context about your project and your capability as a company to successfully execute the program. Given the large number of documents required for submission, it is critical to start early, remain organized, and carefully proofread all the components for content and consistency. Some components will need to be prepared sequentially; others can be prepared in parallel. The recommended timelines in this section take into account these interdependencies, and the total time requirement for preparing your other components is approximately 50 – 100 hours.

Tasks

1. Check company registrations. *(Week 1)*

2. Complete administrative information in the application package. *(Week 2)*

3. Prepare other components. *(Weeks 2-11)*

4. Submit Proposal! *(Week 12)*

Section III - Other Components

1. Check company registrations. (*Week 1*)

You may recall the many days and weeks required to complete all of the necessary registrations prior to submitting your Phase I application. Fortunately, you will not need to replicate that process prior to your Phase II submission! However, several of the required registrations need to be updated annually, and some passwords are only valid for a few months. Therefore, you should systematically check that each of your registrations is up-to-date so that you are ready to go when it is time to submit your proposal.

\>> Check your System for Award Management (SAM) registration at SAM.gov.

☐ Log into SAM to determine when your registration needs to be renewed.

☐ Renew your SAM registration prior to the registration expiration date. If your registration will expire within a few weeks of your Phase II submission date, we recommend renewing it prior to the submission.

☐ To renew your registration, follow the prompts in SAM. There are several companies that offer to renew your SAM registration for you, for a fee, and they may send you spam emails throughout the year. We recommend that you ignore these emails, and instead complete the renewal yourself. As of Spring of 2018, SAM requires a notarized letter to activate new accounts and account renewals. Keep in mind that this extra step lengthens the time it takes to renew your account.

Section III - Other Components

>> Review your Small Business Association (SBA) registration confirmation file.

- If any of your corporate information has changed since your prior submission, such as number of employees or address, update these by logging in to your SBIR.gov account.

- Download your updated SBA registration document and save the PDF. Keep the filename as-is.

>> Review your Grants.gov and eRA Commons accounts.

- Log into your Grants.gov account and update the password if necessary. Ensure you have Authorized Organization Representative (AOR) permission, which is required for submitting the proposal, by checking the "roles" within your account profile.

- Log into both the Signing Official (SO) and Principal Investigator (PI) accounts in eRA Commons and update the passwords if necessary. If your PI has changed since your Phase I submission, you will need to create a new PI account and affiliate it with your company.

2. Complete administrative information in the application package. (*Week 2*)

In addition to the documents that you are preparing for the grant application, there are several administrative items that must be populated online within the application.

Section III - Other Components

There are two options you can use to prepare and submit an application: 1) ASSIST, and 2) Grants.gov Workspace. ASSIST is NIH's web-based service for the preparation, submission, and tracking of grant applications. Workspace is a shared, online system managed by Grants.gov that allows multiple users to simultaneously work on forms within the application. While both options have strengths and weaknesses, we recommend using ASSIST as it allows for more control over editing rights and easy tracking of the application during the submission process. Given our preference for ASSIST, this section of the book is written with the assumption that you will be using ASSIST for the preparation and submission of your Phase II application.

>> Log into ASSIST as the PI or SO.

>> Enter the Funding Opportunity Announcement (FOA) number in the Initiate Application section and click "Go."

- Most Phase II proposals are submitted to the SBIR or STTR Omnibus Solicitation. You may also choose to submit your proposal for a targeted Funding Opportunity.

- The NIH has separate solicitations for projects that include a clinical trial and those that do not, so make sure to enter the appropriate FOA number depending on whether your project includes a clinical trial.

- The NIH has separate FOA numbers for SBIR and STTR proposals. Be sure you enter the proper number based on your program.

Section III - Other Components

☐ Double check all of the information provided for the FOA after you select "Go," particularly the Opportunity Close Date, to ensure that you entered the proper FOA number.

☐ If you have previously used the ASSIST system to submit your Phase I proposal, you can use the "Copy Application" feature. This feature allows you to make a copy of a previous application and then modify it for a current FOA. In order to do this, you will perform an application search instead of initiating a new application. You can search using a variety of identifiers, such as name of the PI, application title, or submission status. Once you select the appropriate application that you want to copy, click "Copy Application" located on the left side of the screen and then enter the FOA number for the new application. The system will transfer all the information and documents from the previous application into the forms for the new FOA. If you use the copy application option, be sure to review all of the information within the application and update information and forms as needed.

\>> Enter your Application Project Title, which should be the same as your Phase I title.

\>> Review the information that is automatically populated for the Applicant Organization, Address, DUNS number, SAM Expiration Date, and Contact PI. Make corrections if necessary.

\>> Click "Initiate Application." A new window will open with several tabs.

\>> Select the "R&R Cover" tab and click "Edit."

Section III - Other Components

☐ Fill out as much of this information as you can by referencing your Phase I application package.

☐ To find the Federal Identifier, check the status page within eRA Commons for your Phase I grant award. Next to the award, you will see several numbers and letters, beginning with a number and the grant activity code (R41 or R43), followed by the IC code and the serial number. In the Federal Identifier field, you will add only the IC code and serial number, which are the letters and numbers that come after the grant activity code. This information is also available on the Summary Statement of your Phase I application. The Federal Identifier will allow the system to link your current application with your previously awarded application.

☐ For "Type of Application," select "New" if this is the first submission of your Phase II application or "Resubmission" if it is the second submission of your Phase II application.

☐ Populate all of the required fields that are indicated with a red asterisk. If you leave any of these fields empty, your application will be flagged with errors.

> **Helpful Hint**
>
> When you click "save" in ASSIST, the top of the page will have red text that indicates what is missing on that page.

☐ The Cover Letter was formerly used to request study section and IC assignments for your application. This information is now included elsewhere in the application, and so you most likely do not need to include a Cover Letter for your Phase II application. Examples of when you need a Cover Letter are to

Section III - Other Components

provide an explanation for a late submission or an explanation of atypical budget items.

>> Select the "Cover Page Supplement" tab and click "Edit."

   □ Review all of the questions, and select the appropriate responses.

   □ You do not need to fill out the Inventions and Patents Section.

>> Select the "Other Project Information" tab and click "Edit."

   □ Click the appropriate boxes in response to each question.

   □ If you are unsure as to whether your project uses Human Subjects, and/or the exemption number, you can visit the website for the Office for Human Research Protections, which is part of the U.S. Department of Health and Human Services, and read their FAQs or walk through their various decision trees to determine how NIH will classify your study.

   □ Upload the Project Summary, Project Narrative, References, Facilities and Other Resources, and Equipment Sections when they are completed.

   □ For "Other Attachments," upload your SBA registration form.

Section III - Other Components

\>\> Select the "Sites" tab.

☐ Under Primary Performance Site, click "Edit" and then on the next page click "Populate from R&R Cover." This will auto-populate with the company address that you provided earlier in the application. Check to be sure it is correct and edit if necessary. Click "Save and Keep Lock" to save the information and return to the Sites overview. Even if your company is virtual, you can list your office address as the main site.

☐ If some of the work will be done through a subaward, add that site as a Project Performance Site. To do this, click "Add Site" and then fill in the required information. You may need to reach out to an administrator at the subaward institution to obtain the necessary information.

\>\> Select the "Sr/Key Person Profile" tab.

☐ Click on "Edit" for the PD/PI and make sure all information is accurate. Instructions for preparing the Biographical Sketch are provided below, and you do <u>not</u> need to include a Current & Pending Support document.

☐ Click on "Add Sr/Key" to add additional Senior and Key Personnel. Enter contact information and upload the Biographical Sketch. Make sure you have an updated Biographical Sketch for each Sr/Key person.

Section III - Other Components

\>> Select the "SBIR/STTR Information" tab.

- Many of the questions in this section are similar to your Phase I proposal, so they should be straightforward to complete.

- Once your Commercialization Plan is finished, save it in PDF format and add it as an attachment.

\>> Complete the Assignment Request Form.

- Select "Add Optional Form" from the menu on the left side of the screen. From the dropdown list, select "Assignment Request Form" and click "Submit Query." You will then notice that an Assignment Request Form has been added to the end of the application tabs.

- Select the "Assignment Request Form" tab and then click "Edit." Enter the Study Section(s) and IC(s) you would like to request for your application. While this is an optional form, it is recommended that you request these assignments. It is likely that your assignments will be the same as they were for your Phase I application.

- Provide the names and affiliations of any individuals whom you do not want to review your application and provide a brief reason for this request (e.g., key personnel of company developing a competing product).

You have now completed the majority of the administrative information required for submission through ASSIST. We have skipped the R&R Budget, Research Plan, and Human Subjects and Clinical Trials tabs, as they will require additional material that will be developed later in the application preparation process. We will revisit each of these three tabs once we discuss these additional materials.

3. Prepare other components. *(Weeks 2-11)*

You can use material from your Phase I submission as a starting point for preparing documents such as Equipment, Facilities and Other Resources, Biographical Sketches, and Project Narrative for your Phase II submission. It is important to update these documents to demonstrate that the company and project have matured since your Phase I submission and that you have the necessary expertise and facilities for the proposed Phase II program. Since several documents can't be completed until after you have finished your Research Plan, it is a good idea to get an early start on as many documents as possible so that you aren't rushed and overwhelmed at the last minute.

a. Budget and Justification

The Phase II budget will be organized in the same categories as the Phase I budget; however, the budget cap for a Phase II award is $1.5 million and the performance period can be up to two years. This cap can be exceeded if your proposed work addresses one of the SBA-approved topics, which are published each year and can be found through a link on the NIH SBIR/STTR website. In addition, some Institutes have stipulations on the total allowed costs per year. Be sure that your budget meets these

Section III - Other Components

stipulations and adjust your performance period or overall costs as needed.

For an SBIR application, 50% of the total budget must be directed to the small business (note that in Phase I, this requirement was 67%). For an STTR application, 40% of the total budget must be directed to the small business, and 30% of the total budget must be directed to the Partnering Research Institute. These requirements must be followed for each project period in your Phase II program.

\>\> Create and Populate a Budget Spreadsheet.

☐ Pulling together all your budget numbers for your Phase II proposal will be much easier if you create a spreadsheet in Excel. Include each budget category in your spreadsheet and use the formula feature to total each budget category separately in addition to providing totals for direct costs, indirect costs, and fee. Use separate sheets for each project period.

☐ Add budgetary items to your spreadsheet, using estimates of project costs from quotations, vendor catalogs, and other sources.

☐ Check the percentage of funds being directed to your business versus external expenses to ensure that you are meeting the appropriate SBIR or STTR requirements.

Section III - Other Components

>> Identify CROs and consultants.

☐ If external work will be performed by CROs, request the necessary quotes. Quotes may need some modifications and may dictate other budget decisions, so it is advisable to request these quotes early.

☐ In a Phase II project, consultant costs will likely be a larger part of the budget than in your Phase I application. Note the hourly rate and number of hours that each consultant will commit to your Phase II project.

>> Request items from subaward institutions.

☐ If your Phase II project includes a subaward, you will need to obtain a budget and Budget Justification from the subaward institution. It is helpful to provide the subawardee's pre-award office with the Subaward Budget form that you can download from ASSIST so that they can return a Subaward Budget to you that is compatible for direct upload into ASSIST.

☐ You will need Biographical Sketches of Key Personnel, facilities and equipment information, vertebrate animals and human subjects information (if applicable), and a letter of intent from the subaward institution.

☐ Subaward items often take some time to generate and obtain; therefore, be sure to notify your subaward institutions of all the documents that are needed in your initial request and follow-up frequently to make sure you obtain all the documents on time.

Section III - Other Components

>> Construct your Budget Justification using your completed budget spreadsheet.

☐ Create a word document that includes a justification for each line item in your budget, similar to your Phase I Budget Justification. You should divide your Budget Justification into project periods (generally 1 year = 1 project period).

☐ Quotes and letters from consultants should be included at the end of the Budget Justification to provide support for those items.

>> Calculate your indirect costs and fee.

☐ As with Phase I, the NIH allows up to a 40% indirect rate without a negotiation. In most cases, a 40% indirect rate is appropriate for a company applying for its first Phase II award. However, if your actual indirect costs are substantial, you may want to consider entering a provisional rate that is higher than 40% in order to trigger an indirect rate negotiation at time of award (for more information, see Section 4).

☐ Request a fee that is 7% of your total (direct + indirect) costs. It is usually advantageous to request the maximum allowable fee, since your company can use these funds for expenses that may not be covered by directs and indirects, such as IP protection and marketing.

Section III - Other Components

\>\> Populate the R&R Budget in ASSIST.

☐ Select the R&R Budget tab and click "Edit." Enter the budget period dates for project period 1 and populate the budget categories as appropriate.

☐ Upload your Budget Justification by selecting "Add Attachment" at the bottom of the page. You will only upload one Budget Justification for the entire project. Although the Budget Justification file is located at the end of project period 1, the information in the file covers the entire project. Select "Save and Keep Lock."

☐ To enter costs for additional project periods, click "Add Period" at the top of the page and then follow instructions given above.

☐ Be sure to confirm you entered the appropriate numbers by checking the ASSIST totals with those from your budget spreadsheet.

b. Biographical Sketches

Once you have identified the key personnel for your proposal, you can start working on their Biographical Sketches. Reviewers will scrutinize these closely to ensure your team has the appropriate expertise. Since you are allowed up to five pages per Biographical Sketch, you should have plenty of space to highlight the strong backgrounds of the investigators and how they will contribute to the success of the project.

Section III - Other Components

\>\> Update the Biographical Sketches for your PI and other Key Personnel from Phase I.

    ☐ Add each Key Personnel's accomplishments from Phase I to their Personal Statements and describe their contribution to Phase II.

    ☐ Update publication lists and Contributions to Science.

    ☐ Be sure to add the Phase I award to Section D of the Biographical Sketch.

\>\> Create Biographical Sketches for any new Key Personnel and consultants.

    ☐ Download the Biographical Sketch template and instructions available from the NIH website and ask the individuals to provide the relevant information.

    ☐ The personal statement should provide a concise description of the individual's expertise and role in the Phase II program.

\>\> Evaluate the Biographical Sketches to determine if any additional Key Personnel are needed.

    ☐ Consider all parts of the Phase II project and make sure there are no gaps in the company's expertise that will be required to successfully execute the proposed program.

- If you identify any gaps in the expertise of the team, locate consultants to fill these gaps and obtain Letters of Support and Biographical Sketches.

c. Letters of Support

You will include several Letters of Support with your Phase II proposal. In addition to the Letters from key opinion leaders, potential partners, and investors to support the content of your Commercialization Plan, you will also need Letters from your consultants and CROs.

>> Request Letters from Consultants.

- Letters from each Consultant should include the title of your Phase II project, a short biographical summary of the consultant, the role the consultant will play in the project, the number of hours the consultant will commit per year of the project, and the hourly rate.

>> Request Letters from CROs.

- Letters from CROs should state the service that will be provided as well as summarize the CRO's expertise to indicate that they are well-suited to perform the proposed study and have the necessary facilities.

- Many CROs have standard Letters that they can modify for your proposal.

d. Project Summary and Narrative

The Project Summary and Narrative should concisely summarize your project. Both documents will be publicly available, so be sure to exclude any proprietary information.

\>\> Write your Project Summary.

- ☐ As for your Phase I application, your Project Summary is limited to 30 lines.

- ☐ Begin your Project Summary with the Significance and Innovation of your project. This can be similar to your Specific Aims page, but should be targeted to a non-expert audience.

- ☐ Highlight the progress that you have made in your Phase I project, and how the Phase II project will further advance your product's development.

- ☐ State your Specific Aims. Highlight any significant components of your project, such as collaboration with a well-known investigator, key milestones you will achieve, and human health impacts that you expect to make.

- ☐ Conclude your Project Summary by restating the value of the project. The conclusion should "pitch" your project to reviewers.

Section III - Other Components

\>> Write your Project Narrative.

☐ Write approximately 2-3 sentences that describe the human health impact of your project.

☐ Your Project Narrative can be exactly the same as your Phase I Narrative, or you can update it to reflect any changes.

e. Facilities and Other Resources and Equipment

Your Facilities and Other Resources and Equipment documents will be very similar to your Phase I proposal.

\>> Update your Facilities and Other Resources and Equipment documents with any changes that have occurred since your Phase I submission.

☐ In addition to a description, pictures may be included to effectively display your facilities.

☐ Include shared spaces that you use and comment on how those environments will contribute to the success of your project.

☐ If you are proposing that significant work will be done by CROs and/or a subaward institution, describe their facilities and available equipment for the project.

☐ If you are using biohazards, include a description of your biosafety practices in your Facilities and Other Resources document.

Section III - Other Components

☐ Ensure that the listed facilities and equipment fully support the execution of the proposed Phase II program.

f. Select Agents, Human Subjects, Vertebrate Animals, Authentication of Key Resources, Resource Sharing Plan, and Multi-PI/PD Leadership Plan

There are several additional documents that may apply to your application, depending on your scope of work. If your Phase II program involves the use of select agents, human subjects, vertebrate animals, and/or key biological/chemical resources, you will need to include additional forms to provide details on the use of these resources in order to meet NIH requirements. Proposals that involve the development of model organisms, generation of large amounts of genomic data, or exceed a specific budget level require a description of means by which data generated from the proposal will be shared with the scientific community. Additionally, projects that involve more than one PI require the submission of a Multi-PI/PD Leadership Plan. Instructions for completing each of these documents are provided below; prepare only those documents that are required for your proposal.

>> Prepare your Select Agents document.

☐ Determine if you are using Select Agents as identified by the Federal Select Agents Program.

☐ The Select Agents document must identify the select agent that will be used, provide the registration status of all entities where the select agent will be used, and provide a description of all facilities where the select agent will be used. In the

Section III - Other Components

facilities description, you must include procedures that will be used to monitor possession and transfer of the agent and plans for biosafety, biocontainment, and security.

>> Prepare Human Subjects information.

☐ For the Human Subjects information, some of the items are uploaded as separate documents, while others are entered into boxes within ASSIST.

☐ If your project involves human specimens and/or data, but does not meet the NIH definition of "human subjects research," you will need to provide a short document titled "Human Subjects" that explains why the application does not involve human subjects. If you are not sure whether your proposed project is human subjects research, the NIH has developed a questionnaire, available online, that can help you make this determination. For projects using de-identified human specimens or data (e.g., from a biorepository or an existing database), generally a paragraph of explanation is sufficient. Make sure to specify that the samples/data you will receive will be de-identified and include the following information, if applicable to your project: name of the biorepository or database; name of its director/manager; location of biorepository; any existing Institutional Review Board (IRB) approvals covering the biorepository; and any information about the donors of specimens (e.g., age, disease state) that you will receive along with the specimens. It is recommended that you also include a Letter of Support from the director/manager of the biorepository or database as

Section III - Other Components

confirmation that the specimens or data will be available for your project.

☐ If your project involves human subjects and is not considered a clinical trial, you will need to provide the following information:

- <u>Name of study</u>: Select a name for the study. Be sure that it enables reviewers to easily cross-reference the study's location in the Research Plan, especially if you have multiple human subject studies in your proposal.

- <u>Focus of study</u>: Briefly describe the purpose of the study.

- <u>Eligibility criteria</u>: Describe the inclusion and exclusion criteria for the study.

- <u>Minimum and maximum ages for enrollment</u>: Specify the required ages.

- <u>Plans for Inclusion of Women, Minorities, and Children</u>: Provide scientific justification of the inclusion or exclusion of women, minorities, and children. This information should be organized using two separate headers, "Inclusion of Women and Minorities" and "Inclusion of Children."

- <u>Recruitment and Retention Plan</u>: Briefly describe how you intend to recruit subjects for the study and any strategies that will be used to ensure that subjects complete the study.

Section III - Other Components

- <u>Study Timeline</u>: Generate a high-level timeline of the proposed study. This can be in paragraph form or a table/figure.

- <u>Date of Enrollment of First Subject</u>: Select the date that you intend to begin enrollment.

- <u>Inclusion Enrollment Report</u>: Populate the provided table with expected population demographics for study.

- <u>Protection of Human Subjects:</u> This is the most important and carefully scrutinized document in your Human Subjects section. The document is typically several pages long and consists of Risks to Human Subjects, Adequacy of Protection Against Risks, Potential Benefits of the Proposed Research to Human Subjects and Others, and Importance of the Knowledge to be Gained. Given the high level of detail that you need to include in this section, we strongly recommend that you carefully read the instructions in the Application Guide to ensure you include all required details. Also, we recommend asking an individual who is familiar with human subjects requirements for NIH projects to review this section of your proposal.

☐ If your proposal is classified as a clinical trial, you will need to provide information in addition to the above items. Refer to the Application Guide for a more detailed description of each component. We provide a high-level overview of these items below:

Section III - Other Components

- Data and Safety Monitoring Plan: Describe what information will be monitored and the overall framework for safety monitoring, including individuals who will be responsible for monitoring, the frequency of the monitoring and plans for interim analysis, and the process by which adverse events and other issues will be reported.

- Overall Structure of the Study Team: Describe the organizational structure of the team for the clinical trial. This should include any of the following that are relevant to the proposed trial: administrative sites, data coordinating sites, enrollment/participating sites, and laboratory/testing centers.

- Brief Summary of Clinical Trial: Summarize objectives of study, including endpoints. The summary is limited to 5,000 characters.

- Narrative of Study Description: Describe the study protocol, including assignment of individuals, delivery of interventions, and statistical design and power.

- Intervention: Provide a name and description for each intervention, limited to 1,000 characters.

- Outcome Measures: For each important measurement, provide a name, the time frame for collection, and a brief description of the metric.

- Statistical Design and Power: State the number of subjects that you anticipate enrolling, the expected effect size, the power, and the statistical methods that will be employed with respect to each outcome measurement that you listed. Justify that your methods for sample size and data analysis are appropriate.

• Participation Duration: Provide the time it will take for an individual participant to complete the study.

• Availability of Investigational Product (IP) and IND/IDE Status: State if the study will include an FDA-regulated intervention. You should describe the availability of the study agents and support for the acquisition and administration of the agents. If applicable, state the IND/IDE status and describe any FDA interactions to-date. Note that some Institutes require that your IND/IDE be submitted at the time of application. It is highly recommended that you check the Institute's guidelines for clinical trials research early in the process for preparing your application so that you can be sure you meet any Institute-specific requirements.

• Dissemination Plan: Describe your plan for dissemination of the clinical trial information. Refer to the NIH website for their policy on "Dissemination of NIH-Funded Clinical Trial Information" and see the Application Guide for specifics on what the plan should address.

>> Prepare the Vertebrate Animals Section.

☐ This document will be used to determine whether your animal experiments are sound; therefore, provide sufficient

Section III - Other Components

detail so that experimental designs can be well understood and ensure that supportive practices are thoroughly described.

☐ Begin the document with the title "Vertebrate Animal Section" and provide a short paragraph that states which facility will perform each of the proposed experiments involving animals.

☐ Include each of the following sections:

• <u>Description of Procedures</u>: Provide a concise description of each experiment involving animals that will be performed. Be sure to include the species, strains, ages, sex, and total numbers. If dogs or cats are being used, you need to include the source of the animals.

• <u>Justifications</u>: Explain why animals must be used and why the experiments can't be conducted using an alternative, non-animal model. Also, support the use of the selected species.

• <u>Minimization of Pain and Distress</u>: Describe procedures that will be executed to minimize discomfort, distress, pain, and injury. These may include analgesia, anesthesia, sedation, and humane endpoints.

>> Prepare the Authentication of Key Biological and Chemical Resources document.

Section III - Other Components

☐ This document is only required if you are using resources that require validation of quality and authenticity prior to use and throughout the proposed program. These items may include (but are not limited to): genetically modified animals, bacterial strains, cell lines, antibodies, and manufactured drug agents. Routine reagents, such as buffers, do not need to be included.

☐ Begin the document with the title "Authentication of Key Biological and Chemical Resources." For each applicable item, list the item and then briefly describe methods that you will undertake to confirm and maintain the validity of these resources.

☐ For resources that undergo quality control checks prior to your purchase, it is not sufficient to simply list the pre-purchase protocols if you will be using the reagent for an extended period of time throughout the program. For example, cell lines that are purchased from a vendor must undergo routine checks for authenticity once they are being used in your facility.

>> Prepare the Resource Sharing Plan.

☐ If any of the following applies to your proposed project, you will need to prepare a Resource Sharing Plan: 1) you are requesting $500,000 or more in direct costs, exclusive of the subaward Facilities and Administrative (F&A) costs, in any budget period; 2) you are proposing to develop model organisms; or 3) you are proposing to generate large-scale genomic data.

Section III - Other Components

☐ The document is divided into three sections:

• <u>Data Sharing Plan</u>: If you are requesting more than $500,000 in a single budget period, you will need to describe how you will facilitate data sharing related to the project. This can involve giving presentations at certain conferences and/or publishing in peer-reviewed journals. The Small Business Act permits SBIR/STTR grantees to withhold data for 4 years after the end of the grant award in order to file patents, which you can state in your plan.

• <u>Sharing Model Organisms</u>: Required for programs that propose to develop a model organism. You should describe the plans for sharing and distributing the model or state why you cannot share. You may reference the Small Business Act as a reason for delaying sharing of information.

• <u>Genomic Data Sharing</u>: If you will generate large amounts of genomic data, you should describe your plans for sharing this information.

>> Prepare the Multi-PI/PD Leadership Plan.

☐ This document is only required for proposals that have multiple Key Personnel who are serving in the role of PI as indicated by selecting "PI" as role on the "Sr/Key Personnel" tab in ASSIST. The decision to have a single PI versus multiple PIs is generally based on experience of the investigators. If your PI has limited experience managing projects similar in scope to what you are proposing, it may be helpful to include another PI with more experience. A Multi-PI arrangement is also common when the expertise of two or more individuals is equally critical to the project.

☐ Title the document "Multi-PI/PD Leadership Plan." The document is usually ½ - 1 page long and should include the following headings and content:

• Rationale for Multiple PI/PD Plan: Describe the expertise of each PI and why a Multi-PI approach is critical to the execution of the program.

• Governance and Structure of the Leadership Team: Describe how often the team will meet to discuss the project and how decisions will be made and agreed upon. Indicate responsibilities for scientific and administrative aspects of the project. Provide procedures for resolving potential conflicts.

4. Submit Proposal! (*Week 12*)

You have finally completed all of the required components for your Phase II proposal and are ready to submit! This section will provide you with an organized approach to completing the submission so that this final task proceeds as smoothly as possible.

>> Compile vendor quotations, Letters of Support, and Biographical Sketches. Do a final check to ensure these documents are completed correctly and that budget items are

Section III - Other Components

consistent with the numbers entered in the budget section of the proposal.

\>\> Put all documents into final format.

☐ Convert all documents to PDF format for upload.

☐ For the Research Plan, separate the Specific Aims, Research Strategy, and References into distinct files. This is easiest to do by first converting the full Research Plan to a PDF and then extracting the necessary pages and renaming them as the appropriate sections.

☐ The NIH does not dictate what formatting option to use for your references. One common option is the standard format used by the National Library of Medicine.

☐ If you are not including the Commercialization Plan references within the Commercialization Plan document, combine the Commercialization Plan references with the Research Plan references.

\>\> Upload remaining documents.

☐ Log into ASSIST using the PI or SO account information. To locate the application that you initiated in Week 2, select "Search for Application" and enter a search element. Select the appropriate application from the search results by selecting "Edit."

Section III - Other Components

☐ Select the "Other Project Information" tab and click "Edit." Scroll to the bottom of the screen and you will see the option to upload your Project Summary, Project Narrative, References Cited, Facilities and Other Resources, and Equipment documents. Upload the final versions of each of these documents by selecting the "Add Attachment" button for the appropriate document. When finished uploading these documents, select "Save and Keep Lock" at the bottom of the page.

☐ Select the "Sr/Key Person Profile" tab. Click "Edit" next to any individuals for whom you need to add Biographical Sketches. Then add the document by selecting "Add Attachment" at the bottom of the page. Once uploaded, click "Save and Keep Lock."

☐ If your proposal includes a subaward, select the "R&R Subaward Budget" tab to upload the budget. If you are submitting an STTR application, this tab will already be available. If you are submitting an SBIR, you will have to add this tab using the "Add Optional Form" action and selecting "R&R Subaward Budget" from the dropdown list. If you provided the subaward institution with the budget form from ASSIST, you can select "Attach Subaward Form" to upload their budget. Prior to doing this, confirm that the subawardee's Budget Justification is attached at the end of project period 1. If the subawardee did not use the R&R Budget form, you can select "Add New Subaward" and populate the budget form as you did for your company's budget.

Section III - Other Components

☐ Select the "Research Plan" tab and click "Edit." On this page you can click the appropriate "Add Attachment" buttons to upload your Specific Aims, Research Strategy, Vertebrate Animals, Select Agents Research, Letters of Support, Resource Sharing Plan, Multi-PI/PD Leadership Plan, and Authentication of Key Biological and Chemical Resources. If you have a letter of intent from a partnering research organization, upload this as a Consortium Agreement. An Introduction is only required if you are preparing a resubmission (see Section 4).

☐ Select the "SBIR/STTR Information" tab and click "Edit." Locate the "Add Attachment" button for the Commercialization Plan and upload the final version of the document.

☐ Select the "Human Subjects and Clinical Trials" tab and click "Edit." Populate the required fields and upload the Human Subject documents as appropriate.

>> Submit the application.

☐ Be sure that you have populated all required fields and have uploaded all documents.

☐ Generate a preview of your application to make sure that you have included the necessary information and that everything looks satisfactory. To generate a preview, select the "Summary" tab and then choose the "Preview Application" action on the left side of the screen. In the new window, click

Section III - Other Components

"Generate Preview." Carefully inspect the preview and return to the application to make any necessary modifications.

☐ To ready the application for submission, select the "Update Submission Status" action. In the new window choose "Ready for Submission" from the dropdown list, then click to continue. The system will check your application for errors and warnings, and you will be notified of the results of this check in a new window. If the application is error-free, the system will allow you to continue to set your proposal to "Ready for Submission." If the system found any errors or warnings, you can select and view these errors and warnings. If you have errors, you must correct them in order to submit the proposal. Once you fix the errors, repeat the steps for setting your application status to "Ready for Submission." If your application has only warnings, your application can be submitted without correction, and you can proceed with the status change by selecting to ignore the warnings.

☐ You must login to the SO account to submit the application. On the "Summary" tab for the application, you will see a "Submit Application" option next to "Status." This button will be active once you set the application to "Ready for Submission." Click "Submit Application" and then enter your Grants.gov AOR account information in the new window. Once the credentials are approved, the "Application Information" window will return and you can select the link for "Check Submission Status" located next to the status category for the application. If you click "Check Submission Status," you will receive updates as the application proceeds through the various steps of the submission process prior to

Section III - Other Components

landing in eRA Commons as an official application. Once a proposal is successfully submitted, you will see "Submitted" for the ASSIST status, "Agency Tracking Number Assigned" for the Grants.gov status, and "Processed" for the Agency status in addition to an agency tracking number. You can click on the agency tracking number to access the complete application in eRA Commons.

☐ Once you submit the application, you have two business days to submit a corrected application if needed (as long as it is prior to the deadline). To submit a corrected application, you will first need to set the application back to a "Work in Progress" by selecting the "Update Submission Status" action and then selecting "Work in Progress" from the dropdown list. This step allows you to modify the proposal. After you complete your corrections, you will need to select the "Changed/Corrected" application box on the "R&R Cover" tab and add the "Previous Grants.gov Tracking ID," which can be found on the "Summary" tab. You can then repeat the process of readying the application for submission.

Once you have carefully reviewed your final submitted proposal, you have officially completed Phase II application process! Now is a good time to take a much needed and deserved break as you prepare for the lengthy review and award process.

Section IV. Review and Award Process

Objectives: Now that you have submitted your Phase II proposal, it is time to start the waiting game. In this section, we will cover the review timeline, the award and resubmission process, and the grants management responsibilities for your new award. We will then conclude this book with a discussion of what your company can expect during the Phase II SBIR/STTR project period and beyond.

Tasks:

1. Undergo the review process.

2. Prepare a resubmission, if necessary.

3. Receive your Notice of Award! Understand your company's Phase II responsibilities.

4. Prepare for "beyond Phase II."

Section IV – Review and Award Process

1. Undergo the review process.

The review process for your Phase II application will be very similar to your experience for your Phase I application. Your submitted application is initially sent to the NIH's Center for Scientific Review (CSR), where a referral officer will assign the application to an SRG and to the appropriate NIH IC. The Scientific Review Officer (SRO) for the SRG will assign the proposal to at least three initial reviewers. Applications that rank in approximately the top half after these initial reviews will be discussed at the study section meeting. During the meeting, the proposal will be assigned a final impact/priority score, and a Summary Statement is prepared that provides a detailed critique of the application. Applications that receive strong scores at the SRG panel meeting will be further discussed at the IC's Advisory Council/Board meeting, to determine the recommendation for funding. Finally, the PO will initiate the award process for successful applications.

Given the complexity of the review process, and the variability in protocols among different ICs, you should feel free to reach out to your SRO (prior to the study section meeting) or PO (after the study section meets) to ask about the status and next steps. Your PO can often provide insight beyond what you obtain from reading the IC's publicly available information about its review process.

An approximate timeline of key milestones during the review process is provided below:

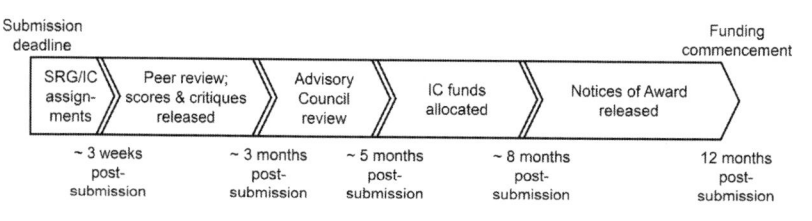

Submission deadline					Funding commencement
SRG/IC assignments	Peer review; scores & critiques released	Advisory Council review	IC funds allocated	Notices of Award released	
~ 3 weeks post-submission	~ 3 months post-submission	~ 5 months post-submission	~ 8 months post-submission	12 months post-submission	

Section IV – Review and Award Process

\>\> Receive your SRG and IC assignments.

☐ Approximately 2-3 weeks after submitting your proposal, you will receive SRG and IC assignments. In some cases, you may receive an email notification of the assignments; in other cases, you will need to log into eRA Commons and select the appropriate application number to view your SRG and IC assignments.

☐ It is likely that your SRG and IC assignments for Phase II are the same as for your Phase I proposal. If there is a new SRG assignment, it is possible that the SRGs have been reorganized since your Phase I submission. You can review the scope of the new SRG as well as prior meeting rosters on the NIH's SBIR/STTR Study Sections website.

☐ If you feel that the assigned SRG is not appropriate for your proposal and would like to request reassignment, contact the SRO who is associated with your proposal in eRA Commons.

☐ If you feel the IC assignment is not appropriate, or if you feel that additional ICs should be considered for secondary assignments, contact the Division of Receipt and Referral (DRR). While most SBIR/STTRs are funded by the primary IC, assignment to a secondary IC can be advantageous since it provides additional possible funding sources for your project. Keep in mind that an IC can only fund proposals to which it is assigned.

☐ In our experience, you will need a very strong justification for your IC or SRG assignment to be changed. If you want to

Section IV – Review and Award Process

request a reassignment, it is important that you contact the SRO or DRR as soon as possible once the initial assignments are released, since the change is more difficult to make once the proposal has been assigned to the primary reviewers.

>> Obtain your final impact score and Summary Statement.

☐ Several weeks after you receive your SRG assignment, the panel review date will be posted in eRA Commons. In some instances, the SRO will send an email to all applicants notifying them of the panel review and explaining the review process. In other cases, you will need to check the eRA Commons website to see if the panel review date has been posted.

☐ Your final impact score will be posted within three business days of completion of the panel review. As with your Phase I application, the impact score will range from 10 to 90, or you will receive a result of "Not Discussed" if your application was not reviewed during the panel discussion.

☐ Your Summary Statement will be posted in eRA Commons approximately three weeks after you receive your impact score.

>> Discuss your Summary Statement with your PO.

☐ Prior to contacting your PO, carefully review your Summary Statement. Read the panel review as well as the individual reviewers' comments. Note the reviewers' perceived strengths and weaknesses.

Section IV – Review and Award Process

☐ Prepare responses to all reviewer critiques. Responses to critiques usually fall into one of three categories:

- You agree with the reviewers and are able to modify your proposal to address the concern. This may require completing additional preliminary studies.

- You disagree with the reviewers, and you can provide evidence to support your arguments.

- You realize that you did not provide enough information for reviewers to appropriately evaluate your project, and you can provide this additional information to allay their concerns.

☐ Prior to talking with your PO, draft responses to the critiques so that you are prepared to discuss them with your PO.

☐ Reach out to your PO via email and request to discuss your Summary Statement. Be sure to list the application number in the subject line of the email, so that the PO knows what proposal you are referring to. It is always best to ask for a phone call, and most POs will be happy to speak with you. Keep in mind that some POs have very busy schedules, so it may take several weeks to schedule the call.

☐ You will get the most out of your call with your PO by asking questions, so that you can obtain his/her expert insight. The following are good questions to ask:

Section IV – Review and Award Process

- *What is your assessment of the strengths and weaknesses of my application?* It is easy for you to get caught in a trap of focusing too much of your attention on relatively minor reviewer critiques. Your PO can assist you in determining the score-driving strengths and weaknesses of your application.

- *What is your assessment of my response to the reviewers' critiques?* In a non-defensive way, describe how you would address the critiques raised in the Summary Statement and ask your PO whether these responses appropriately address the concerns.

- *What is the probability of funding?* Don't be afraid to ask directly whether the PO feels the application will be competitive for funding. If the PO does not feel the application will be competitive, ask what impact scores are currently being considered for funding, so that you know how close you are.

- *Can you provide some specific guidance on next steps?* Your PO may suggest a resubmission, or may recommend that you wait a few weeks so that s/he can provide further information on whether the current application will likely be funded. In some cases, POs may request that you prepare a 2-3 page rebuttal outlining your responses to reviewers that they can take to the Advisory Council/Board meeting.

☐ Follow up as quickly as possible on any action items from the call. If your PO indicates that your application is competitive for funding, continue to reach out to your PO at regular intervals to check on the status.

2. Prepare a resubmission, if necessary.

If your application received a score of "Not Discussed," or if your PO has indicated that your impact score is not strong enough for your proposal to be considered for funding, you are in the unfortunate scenario of needing to resubmit your Phase II proposal. It is important to understand that you are allowed only one resubmission of your Phase II proposal. In contrast to an unfunded Phase I, you cannot submit a "new" Phase II proposal after you have completed a submission and resubmission. Therefore, you should ensure that your Phase II resubmission is as strong as possible, or you risk losing the opportunity to obtain this follow-on SBIR/STTR funding for your Phase I project.

\>\> Develop a strategy for your resubmission.

☐ The timing of your resubmission can be critical. For business reasons, it is desirable to receive the Phase II funding as quickly as possible, so you may be motivated to resubmit right away. However, since only one resubmission is allowed for each original application, you should take the time to address all reviewer concerns from your first submission. If the reviewers noted gaps in your preliminary data, it is to your advantage to complete additional studies prior to your resubmission. If the reviewers' comments can be addressed easily through further clarification of key points, then you may be able to resubmit relatively quickly.

Section IV – Review and Award Process

☐ In order to address reviewers' concerns with the Research Strategy, you may need to provide additional details in the Approach section, perform supplementary studies, or propose additional work to be conducted during Phase II. Discussions with consultants and your team will help to outline the steps needed to fill the reviewers' perceived holes in your Research Strategy and to strengthen the presentation.

☐ Often reviewer critiques can be addressed through bringing on additional experts who can help validate your value proposition or any perceived weakness. You may consider new employees, consultants, or advisors to help fill these roles. Make sure you pay equal attention to building your scientific, business, regulatory, and other specialized competencies that are critical to your company's overall research program and commercial development.

☐ It is always helpful to have third-party experts provide Letters of Support for the claims that you make in your proposal. This is particularly important for content for which there is not readily available peer-reviewed literature to support your claims. Examples where additional Letters of Support can be valuable are: validating a market for a new product; providing clinician or end-user opinions about your product; or addressing specific reviewer concerns.

☐ Several months have likely passed since your initial Phase II submission. Reviewers will expect that your business plan will have evolved during this time, and you should provide updates to reviewers on any changes to your business strategy.

Section IV – Review and Award Process

☐ Once you have developed a plan for addressing the reviewer critiques, send your PO a summary of your strategy. Your PO can provide valuable feedback to ensure you are on the right track.

>> Prepare the one-page Introduction, which is your opportunity to respond to reviewer critiques from your first submission.

☐ Begin with a short statement thanking reviewers for their evaluation of your Phase I project.

☐ Summarize the major reviewer critiques in an introductory paragraph. State that although you do not have room to comment on all critiques within the 1-page limit of the Introduction, you will address the major ones here, and that you have made revisions throughout the proposal to address all critiques.

☐ List approximately 4-8 of the most significant critiques, and provide a brief description of how you have addressed them in the resubmission. Mention additional supporting documentation, preliminary studies, or other work you have assembled to properly address all critiques.

>> Make appropriate edits throughout all documents in your resubmission application, to ensure you have responded to all of the reviewers' critiques.

☐ Indicate substantial changes in your Research Plan and other documents by highlighting, underlining, or using a different text color.

□ Include the additional supporting information that you have gathered, such as Letters of Support, and provide updated vendor quotes.

□ Ensure that your documents are consistent. For example, if you adjusted a vertebrate animal study in your Research Plan, make sure you revise your Vertebrate Animal Section as well.

\>\> Upload your resubmission application in ASSIST and submit.

□ Refer to instructions in Section III of this book for how to use the Copy Application feature of ASSIST. This will allow you to copy the application from your first submission of your Phase II to be used for your resubmission. Be sure to change your project period, replace any documents with newer versions, upload your Introduction, and make any additional changes as needed. In addition to the modifications that came along with addressing reviewer comments, you will also need to change the type of application within the "R&R Cover" tab from new to resubmission.

3. Receive your Notice of Award! Understand your company's Phase II responsibilities.

If your proposal is being considered for funding, you will receive a Just-in-Time (JIT) request from a Grants Management Specialist (GMS). While a JIT request does not guarantee an award, it is a good sign that the Institute is considering funding your application! Upon successful completion of the JIT process, you will receive a Notice of Award (NOA), at which time you will be responsible for overseeing a >$1M Phase II budget. It is

Section IV – Review and Award Process

therefore important to understand the requirements for proper stewardship of the Government's substantial investment in your company.

>> Prepare your JIT documentation. Many of these documents will be familiar from the Phase I JIT process, but the GMS will likely require more detailed information about your financial controls. The NIH has become increasingly stringent in recent years to ensure you have all of the appropriate systems and financial controls in place to properly manage the award, so it is important to carefully prepare all requested JIT information. There is often a very short turnaround time for the JIT documents, and it is critical that you communicate with the GMS and supply the required information as quickly as possible. If you are unable to obtain a required document in time, notify the GMS early and provide an estimated time for when you will be able to obtain it. If you know that a JIT request is imminent, you can start assembling the following documents:

☐ SBIR or STTR Funding Agreement Certification

☐ SBIR or STTR Life Cycle Certification

☐ Justification of Foreign Components

☐ Financial Questionnaire and Evaluation of Financial Management Systems, including:

- Copies of the latest Balance Sheet and Income Statement

- Description of the administrative capability of your organization, including the existence and substance of (a)

Section IV – Review and Award Process

accounting procedures and internal controls; (b) guidelines on salaries/wages and fringe benefits; (c) time and effort reporting; and (d) purchasing procedures.

☐ Certifications:

- Institutional Animal Care and Use Committee (IACUC) Approval Date

- Human Subjects Assurance

- IRB Approval

- Animal Welfare Assurance

☐ Other Support Information for all key personnel

☐ Negotiated Facilities and Administrative (F&A) Cost Agreement

>> If all goes well, within a few weeks of submitting your JIT information, you will **receive your NOA!** Take a moment to congratulate yourself and your team for all your hard work and achievement!

>> Carefully read the NOA in its entirety. The NOA contains critical information about the terms of your grant.

☐ If there are any sections of the NOA that are unclear, you should direct administrative and budget questions to your GMS and research questions to your PO. If you are uncertain

Section IV – Review and Award Process

who to contact, you can send an email to both your GMS and PO.

☐ Your NOA may contain certain conditions that must be met prior to conducting portions of the study (such as the Office of Laboratory Animal Welfare (OLAW) or IRB approval), and it is important that you follow all guidelines and restrictions in your NOA. For example, if you conduct human subjects or animal tests prior to obtaining approval from the NIH, you may not be able to use grant funds to reimburse these costs.

>> Review your Grants Management and Accounting protocols so that you are audit-ready. If you don't have internal expertise in Grants Management, consider engaging an outside resource to ensure you have everything in proper order. Controls that must be in place include:

☐ <u>Policies & Procedures manual</u>. Make sure you have policies in place to address each of the following:

- Asset management

- Billing system

- Cost tracking and allowability

- Delegation of signing authority and review

- Invention disclosure and reporting

- Purchasing

Section IV – Review and Award Process

- Record keeping

- Segregation of duties

- Timekeeping

☐ <u>Accounting system.</u> Make sure your accountant implements each of the following requirements:

- Project cost accounting

- Identifying and appropriately recording direct, indirect, and unallowable expenses

- Documentation to support drawdowns

- Appropriate allocation of employee and contractor time

\>\> Complete Quarterly Federal Financial Reports (FFRs)

☐ The FFR accounts for the financial expenditures on each award to substantiate and validate the funding requested from the Payment Management System (PMS) and is required to be filed within 30 days of the end of each calendar year quarter.

☐ You must identify the direct costs incurred within a quarter on each Federal award. In addition, the indirect and fee percentages are applied to the identified direct costs.

Section IV – Review and Award Process

\>\> File the Annual Report on Possible Research Misconduct.

☐ All institutions are required to establish and renew their research misconduct assurance by annually submitting a report to the Office of Research Integrity (ORI). The report must be submitted between January 1st and April 30th of each calendar year.

☐ For Small Organizations (10 or fewer employees), the ORI accepts the "Small Organization Statement for Handling Allegations of Research Misconduct Involving Public Health Services Research and Related Activities" in lieu of a customized policy.

\>\> Complete the Interim/Annual Research Performance Progress Reports (RPPR)

☐ RPPRs document the research accomplishments and compliance with terms of the award. The Public Health Service (PHS) estimates it will take approximately 15 hours to complete the Progress Report.

☐ Your NOA will note whether your project is eligible for Streamlined Non-Completing Award Process (SNAP) RPPRs. Annual SNAP RPPRs are due approximately 45 days before the next budget period start date. Annual non-SNAP RPPRs are due approximately 60 days before the next budget period start date.

☐ Interim and Final RPPRs are due 120 days from the period of performance end date.

Section IV – Review and Award Process

\>\> Prepare for an audit.

☐ Once your company draws down a certain threshold of government funding (currently $750K) from the PMS in a single fiscal year, your company is required to obtain an external audit.

☐ Locate an auditor with experience in auditing SBIR/STTR funded companies.

☐ You will need to budget approximately $10,000 – $20,000 for the audit, depending on the complexity of your financials.

☐ Determine if you are eligible for a Program-specific Audit, which is typically a less expensive option than a Generally Accepted Government Auditing Standards (GAGAS), or "Yellow Book," audit. The Program-specific audit focuses on internal controls and compliance requirements and less on company financial statements. If you are unsure of your eligibility for this type of audit, you can reach out to the Office of Audit Services.

\>\> Consider negotiating your indirect rate.

☐ The NIH allows SBIR/STTR awardees to receive up to a 40% indirect rate without a negotiation. A Grants Accountant who is familiar with indirect rates can review your financials to determine whether your actual indirect rate may be higher than the 40% threshold.

☐ In order to apply for a higher indirect rate, you will need to "trigger" an indirect rate negotiation. In most cases, you will

Section IV – Review and Award Process

have to apply for a new SBIR/STTR grant award and insert a provisional rate that is greater than 40% in order to trigger this negotiation. Alternatively, if you are being considered for an award for a non-SBIR/STTR grant (such as an R01), you may automatically trigger a negotiation.

☐ An indirect rate negotiation can take several months and will involve a lot of back-and-forth communication with Defense Finance and Accounting Services (DFAS). However, this may very well be worth the effort if it ends up generating several hundred thousand dollars of additional income for your company through the higher indirect funds you will receive with your awards.

4. Prepare for "beyond Phase II."

Despite all the hard work you have done to-date, the reality is that your Phase II award is just the beginning of your journey to commercialize your product! Your Phase II grant will likely provide funding to complete important development work, but you will need to seek additional funds to complete the commercialization effort. Once your financing strategy is in place, it is time to execute the strategy presented in your Commercialization Plan and ultimately bring your innovative technology to market.

>> Seek sources for additional capital.

☐ Grant funding

- Phase IIb. If you have previously been awarded a Phase II proposal for development of your product and met the proposed development milestones, you may be eligible to submit a Phase IIb proposal to support further development of the technology. The Phase IIb mechanism serves to address the "Valley of Death" funding gap between the Phase II award and product commercialization. This mechanism is often used to support IND-enabling studies and clinical trials to achieve regulatory approval.

- Administrative Supplement. If you incur unanticipated additional costs as you conduct your Phase II work, you can discuss applying for an Administrative Supplement with your PO. Although Administrative Supplements are rare, it is worthwhile to discuss the option with your PO.

- Phase I, Fast-Track, or Direct-to-Phase II SBIR/STTR Grants. If your company is interested in pursuing multiple distinct products (such as developing a core technology for different therapeutic indications), you may apply for a new Phase I, Fast-Track, or Direct-to-Phase II SBIR/STTR. Make sure that your new application meets the Phase I criterion of having a new innovation, and that is it not just a second generation of your existing product that is being developed with the current Phase II SBIR/STTR funds.

- Other NIH Grant Mechanisms. Each NIH Institute has multiple funding mechanisms outside of the SBIR/STTR program to advance product development. These may include clinical trial grants, contracts, and free services.

Section IV – Review and Award Process

Other grant mechanisms can be found on the IC web pages or Grants.gov.

- <u>Grants Outside of the NIH</u>. Your technology may be of interest to multiple government agencies, such as the Department of Defense (DoD), the National Science Foundation (NSF), or the United States Department of Agriculture (USDA). You can contact POs at each of these agencies to gauge their potential interest in your technology.

☐ <u>Equity Funding</u>. As an SBIR/STTR awardee, you statistically have a much better chance of receiving equity funding than non-awardees. The NIH reports that between 1992 and 2005, at least 50 of the 200 most frequent SBIR/STTR awardees have received venture funding totaling $1.5 billion. While private investments will require you to give up some ownership of your company, equity funding can be an excellent mechanism for securing financing that will enable you to rapidly accelerate your development and commercialization efforts.

☐ <u>Licensing or Partnership Fees.</u> Once you start making traction with potential partners, you may be able to form a partnership in which certain development milestones trigger payments. You may have to provide a potential partner with exclusivity, so make sure you enter into these agreements carefully, under the guidance of an attorney who is experienced in these negotiations.

Section IV – Review and Award Process

>> Commercialize your product!

Although Phase II/IIb mechanisms are the final opportunities to receive SBIR/STTR grant funding for your product development, "Phase III" is officially the final stage prior to graduating from the SBIR/STTR program. The SBA defines Phase III as the commercialization phase of your product development lifecycle. During this exciting Phase III period, you should have solved most of the uncertainties associated with R&D and be defining a clear and direct path to market.

Seeing your product hit the market can feel surreal, knowing all the hurdles that you have overcome along the way. More importantly, you will see the direct impact that your technology has on improving people's lives. Suddenly, the years of hard work, setbacks, and persistence that you invested in developing your product are all worth it!

Congratulations on completing this journey!

GLOSSARY OF ABBREVIATIONS

ACF	Administration for Children and Families
AOR	Authorized Organization Representative
ASSIST	Application Submission System and Interface for Submission Tracking
CDC	Centers for Disease Control and Prevention
CFO	Chief Financial Officer
cGLP	Current Good Laboratory Practice
cGMP	Current Good Manufacturing Practice
CRO	Contract Research Organization
CSR	Center for Scientific Review
CV	Curriculum Vitae
DRR	Division of Receipt and Referral
DUNS	Data Universal Numbering System
eRA	Electronic Research Administration
F&A	Facilities and Administrative
FDA	Food and Drug Administration
FFR	Federal Financial Report
FOA	Funding Opportunity Announcement
FTO	Freedom to Operate
GAGAS	Generally Accepted Government Auditing Standards
GMS	Grants Management Specialist
IC	Institute/Center
IACUC	Institutional Animal Care and Use Committee
IDE	Investigational Device Exemption
IND	Investigational New Drug
IP	Intellectual Property
IRB	Institutional Review Board
JIT	Just-in-Time
KOL	Key Opinion Leader
NAP	Niche Assessment Program
NIH	National Institutes of Health

NOA	Notice of Award
OLAW	Office of Laboratory Animal Welfare
ORI	Office of Research Integrity
P&L	Profit and Loss
PD	Program Director
PHS	Public Health Service
PI	Principal Investigator
PMS	Payment Management System
PO	Program Officer
R&R	Research and Related
ROI	Return on Investment
RePORT	Research Portfolio Online Reporting Tools
RPPR	Research Performance Progress Report
SAM	System for Award Management
SBA	Small Business Administration
SBDC	Small Business Development Center
SBIR	Small Business Innovative Research
SBTDC	Small Business and Technology Development Center
SNAP	Streamlined Non-Completing Award Process
SO	Signing Official
SRG	Scientific Review Group
SRO	Scientific Review Officer
STTR	Small Business Technology Transfer
TPP	Target Product Profile

INDEX

Advisory Council, 80, 84

Application Guide, vi, 2, 3, 11, 31, 44, 67, 69

Application Package, 3, 34, 46, 48, 51

Approach, iv, v, 36, 39, 40, 44, 86

Assignment Request Form, 54

Audits, 91, 94

Authentication of Key Resources, 64, 70, 71, 76

Authorized Organization Representative (AOR), 48, 77

Biographical Sketch, ii, 55, 57, 59, 60, 61, 73, 75

Budget, ii, iii, 31, 52, 55, 56, 57, 58, 59, 64, 71, 72, 75, 88, 90, 93, 94

Budget Justification, 57, 58, 59, 75

Center for Scientific Review (CSR), 80

Clinical Trials, i, 6, 15, 19, 49, 66, 67, 68, 69, 96

Commercialization Plan, 1, 2, 3, 6, 7, 8, 9, 11, 12, 14, 27, 28, 29, 46, 61, 74, 76, 95

Consultants, 7, 16, 33, 34, 57, 58, 61, 86

Contract Research Organizations (CROs), vi, 31, 33, 57, 61, 63

Cover Page Supplement, 52

Customer, 19, 20, 21, 26

Direct Costs, 56, 71, 92

DUNS Number, 50

Environment, iv, v

Equipment, 52, 55, 63, 75

eRA Commons, 48, 51, 78, 81, 82

Facilities, 52, 55, 63, 71, 75

Fast-Track, iii, iv, 96

Federal Identifier, 51

Fee, 47, 56, 58, 92

Finance Plan, 7, 11, 22

Grants Management Specialist (GMS), 88, 89, 90, 91

Grants.gov, 48, 49, 77, 78, 97

Human Subjects, 52, 55, 64, 65, 67, 76, 90

Impact Score, 82, 85

Indirect Costs, 56, 58

Innovation, i, iv, v, 34, 36, 38, 39, 62

Institute/Center, 31, 51, 54, 80, 81, 96

Institutional Animal Care and Use Committee (IACUC), 90

Institutional Review Board (IRB), 91

Intellectual Property (IP), 21, 22, 58, 69

Investigators, iv, v, 15

Letters of Support, i, ii, vi, 3, 4, 5, 6, 19, 22, 24, 34, 61, 73, 76, 86, 88

Market, v, vi, 1, 6, 7, 8, 9, 10, 13, 18, 19, 20, 21, 26, 28, 35, 37, 86, 95, 98

Multi-PI/PD Leadership Plan, 64, 72, 73, 76

National Institutes of Health (NIH), i, iv, vi, 3, 8, 31, 34, 39, 49, 52, 55, 58, 60, 64, 69, 74, 80, 81, 89, 91, 94, 96, 97

NIH RePORTER, 31

Notice of Award (NOA), 88, 90, 91

Patents, 21, 22, 35

Principal Investigator, 48, 49, 50, 53, 60, 64, 72, 73, 74, 76

Program Officer (PO), i, 80, 82, 83, 84, 85, 87, 90, 91, 96

Progress Report, ii, v, 30, 39, 40, 41, 42, 43, 93

Project Narrative, 52, 55, 62, 63, 68, 75

Project Summary, 40, 52, 62, 75

References, 3, 18, 34, 41, 74

Registrations, 47, 48, 64

Research and Related (R&R) Cover, 50, 53, 78, 88

Research and Related (R&R) Subaward Budget, 75

Research Plan, vi, 13, 29, 30, 31, 32, 33, 44, 45, 46, 55, 66, 74, 76, 87, 88

Research Strategy, ii, 30, 36, 43, 74, 76, 86

Resubmission, 3, iii, 79, 84, 85, 87, 88

Review Process, 3, iv, 79, 80, 82

SBA Registration Form, 52

SBIR/STTR Information Form, 3, 54, 76

Scientific Review Group (SRG), iv, 35, 80, 81, 82

Scientific Review Officer (SRO), 80, 81, 82

Select Agents, 64

Senior/Key Personnel, 53, 60, 72

Significance, iv, v, 13, 34, 36, 37, 38, 62

Signing Official (SO), 48, 49, 74, 77

Small Business Association (SBA), 48, 52, 55, 98

Specific Aims, ii, 5, 30, 35, 36, 40, 44, 62, 74, 76

Subaward Letter of Intent, 57

Subawards, 53, 57, 63, 71, 75

Subcontractors, 31, 33

Submission, iii, vii, 35, 41, 47, 49, 50, 77, 78, 85, 88, 96

Summary Statement, 32, 51, 82

System for Award Management (SAM), 47, 50

Vertebrate Animals, 43, 57, 64, 76

Made in the USA
Coppell, TX
09 July 2024